Coping with Korea

Coping with Korea

Gary P. Steenson

Basil Blackwell

Copyright © Gary P. Steenson 1987

First published 1987

Basil Blackwell Ltd
108 Cowley Road, Oxford, OX4 1JF, UK

Basil Blackwell Inc.
432 Park Avenue South, Suite 1503
New York, NY 10016, USA

British Library Cataloguing in Publication Data

Steenson, Gary P.
    Coping with Korea.
    1. Korea (South)—Description and
    travel—Guide-books
    I. Title
    915.19'50443   DS902.4
ISBN 0–631–15033–1
ISBN 0–631–15622–4 Pbk

Library of Congress Cataloging in Publication Data

Steenson, Gary P., 1944–
    Coping with Korea.

    Includes index.
    1. Korea (South)—Description and travel—Guide-books.
    I. Title.
    DS902.4.S75   1987   915.19'50443   87–10296
ISBN 0–631–15033–1
ISBN 0–631–15622–4 (pbk.)

Typeset in 10 on 11½ pt Garamond
by Opus, Oxford
Printed in Great Britain by Billing & Sons Ltd, Worcester

Contents

General information

The Korean peninsula extends southeast from a border with Manchuria and Siberia for a distance of nearly 960 km; it is about 200 km wide at its widest point. The peninsula has an artificial division at about the midway point from north to south, which separates it into two political entities: the Democratic People's Republic of Korea to the north and the Republic of Korea to the south.

The Republic, more commonly referred to as South Korea, comprises an area of approximately 97,300 square km, slightly larger than Portugal and a bit smaller than the American state of Virginia. Besides the North, South Korea's closest neighbors are China, some 95 km to the west at its closest point across the Yellow Sea, and Japan, almost 200 km to the east of the peninsula across the Sea of Japan (called the East Sea by Koreans).

South Korea itself is very mountainous, being roughly divided into a smaller eastern portion and a slightly larger western portion by mountain ranges. In the east, the mountains fall quickly away to the ocean, creating a rugged coastline with a few isolated small islands. The south and west are not quite as rugged, and contain significant tracts of cultivated, usually rice-producing, land.

Ethnically, Korea is perhaps the most uniform country in the world. It is populated almost exclusively by a single racial-ethnic group, calling themselves the Han, all of whom speak the same Ural-Altaic language. There is a very small, statistically insignificant, Chinese minority, and hardly anyone else. The South has a population of nearly 40 million; the North not quite half that number. South Korea is one of the most densely populated countries in Asia, and ranks fifteenth in population density among all the countries of the world.

Economic background South Korea is a capitalistic state with a very large amount of central government regulation; the financial sector is especially closely controlled by the government. Domestic industries are protected by high tariffs on foreign goods, and those producing for export are encouraged by favorable loan rates and other supports. Free organization of labor is not allowed. Large conglomerates called *chaebol* – including the super conglomerates of Hyundai, Samsung and Daewoo – dominate the economy. The division of the country in 1945 into North and South generally left the North with a wealth of natural resources – especially coal, iron ore and hydroelectric potential – and the South with people and agriculture.

Political and administrative divisions In political terms, South Korea is a republic with an indirectly elected president, selected by an electoral college, and a democratically elected national assembly that also has some appointed members. Provincial and city governments are appointed by the central government. The last two presidents of the South have first seized power in military coups, and then been ratified in office by popular vote after the fact. The present constitution gives the president extraordinary powers not generally considered consistent with a republican form of government.

Administratively, the Republic is made up of nine provinces – Kangwon, Kyonggi, North and South Chungchong, North and South Cholla, North and South Kyongsang and the island of Cheju – plus the five autonomous cities of Seoul, Pusan, Taegu, Inchon and Kwangju. Seoul is one of the five or six largest cities in the world with nearly ten million people.

Climate Normally South Korea has a short (six weeks or so), humid summer and a long, cold and very dry winter; spring, especially in the northern portion of the Republic, can be quite windy and dusty, but the fall is often long and lovely. Nearly all precipitation comes in July and August; winter snowfall is usually quite light. The southern end of the peninsula experiences at least one or two tropical storms or typhoons each

year in the late summer or early fall with very high
winds and torrential rainfall.

History, culture and language

Getting by in South Korea, as in most countries, is largely a matter of being able to anticipate potential differences of perception and behavior, and then minimizing their impact. The vast majority of visitors to a country like Korea never have serious problems because they come into contact with people who have considerable experience dealing with foreigners. But for those visitors who stay longer, or delve deeper, Korea can be a very confusing place.

The language, culture, food, patterns of behavior, and many other aspects of Korea are strange to most westerners. In order to cope with this new place one must know a bit about its history, culture and language. With this background, the newcomer can make more sense of specific situations and avoid possible embarrassment and even offense.

Country name

One very common nickname for the country is 'Land of the Morning Calm'; a visit of a week or two will demonstrate why this is appropriate.

Korea's real name is derived from an old dynastic name, Koryo (itself a shortened form of the even older name, Koguryo); the Koryo ruled much of the peninsula from 936 to 1392. During most of the nineteenth and the early part of the twentieth centuries, the country was called Chosun, the Korean name for the ruling dynasty which is usually called the Yi in the West.

Influence of foreign powers

Korea is an ancient country with an identifiable history at least 3,000 years long. Perhaps the most important feature of its history has been its geographical location. China to the east and Japan to the west have through the millennia fought many wars with each other and against Korea. This has led to the

Korean peninsula often being invaded and conquered, and thus heavily influenced by its two larger neighbors. In fact, so often has Korea been affected by the other two northeast Asian countries that Koreans have a saying which summarizes how they feel about their vulnerability: 'When the whales struggle, the shrimp's back is broken.' Korea has on many occasions been the shrimp that has been crushed by the whales, which are the larger, more powerful nations struggling with each other.

Except for a brief period during the Korean War, Japan has played a more prominent role in Korea than has China during the past hundred years. Unfortunately, Japan's role has not been a benevolent one, and 40 years of occupation of Korea by the Japanese (from 1905 to 1945) left a legacy of distrust and dislike between the two peoples. Japan's rapid economic recovery from the Second World War, and the continued poverty of Korea until the mid-1960s, exacerbated the hostility of Koreans for Japanese. A continuing heavy reliance on Japan for both imports and exports has done little to lessen this hostility.

Anti-Japanese feelings are still very strong in Korea. Among those old enough to remember the Japanese occupation, these sentiments are palpable. Among students, who have as their models and idols the heroic student rebels against Japanese rule of the early years of this century, anti-Japanese feelings are as widespread as any youthful passion. Finally, what many Koreans see as the continued discrimination by Japan against Korean people who reside in the Land of the Rising Sun serves as a constant reminder of the old days of domination.

Prior to the modern era, China was the most powerful influence in Korea. Traditional Korean arts were most strongly influenced by China, Korea's social order is to a great extent still based on the doctrines of Confucius imported from China over a thousand years ago, and South Korea still uses a great many Chinese characters in its written language. But in recent years the United States has largely taken over China's former role as protector of, and major influence upon, Korea. This change came about, of course, as a result of the Korean War, where the country was once again the pawn of great power struggles rather than exclusive master of its own fate.

The influence of the United States in Korea has taken a rather different course from that of China. Whereas China largely had an impact on Korea's culture and social organization, America has influenced Korea's economy, political and military forms. Of course American culture has also had an impact on Korea, especially in movies, music, dress and other popular forms. But these American influenced forms have been little incorporated into traditional Korean culture, standing rather as an alternative culture within the country.

While it is possible to generalize about the attitude of Koreans toward Japan, generalizing about feelings toward the United States is a little more difficult. For a great many South Koreans – those who remember the Korean War – America is still seen as a savior and staunch friend. Most Koreans consider the continuing presence of American troops in their country as a necessity and the best guarantee of continued independence and prosperity. Fear of North Korea is a powerful emotion, especially in Seoul, and very few Koreans would be willing to confront the North militarily without the support of the United States.

However, once the so-called economic miracle of the sixties and the seventies brought prosperity to a great many people, the dominant attitude toward the United States began to change. Once marked by almost unquestioned admiration and gratitude, feelings toward the United States have become more complicated. Korea and America now compete economically; Korea continues to want the United States to be a market for Korean goods, but is less willing to receive American goods. New-found independence has shown Koreans that what is good for the United States is not necessarily or automatically good for Korea.

Politically the country has matured a great deal in the past 30 years, and maturity has brought the freer expression of a broader range of opinion on all topics, including the relationship with the United States. As late as the mid-seventies, questioning the American connection was limited to a radical fringe; in the eighties, discussion of the question has gained some legitimacy. Although there is still no serious movement which advocates severing the relationship completely, more and more Koreans can conceive of the country making its way on the international scene without dependence on the United States.

One constant source of aggravation for Korean–American relations is the presence on the peninsula of more than 30,000 American troops. Despite the fact that most Koreans recognize the necessity of having American troops present, actually seeing and having to deal with them often creates tension and even violence.

Most of the American troops in Korea are young men away from home for the first time; they are often lonely and vulnerable and difficult to control. They occasionally engage in riotous and childish activities that offend Korean standards; usually without malice, of course, but nonetheless with awkward and sometimes serious consequences. The presence in the neighborhood of American bases of prostitutes and bars increases the potential for uncomfortable situations. Resentment among Koreans of fraternization between Korean females and American soldiers is an especially explosive source of difficulties.

Many Koreans, particularly the political opposition and student movements, suffer, to some extent, from what might be called a 'big brother' syndrome in their view of the role of America on the peninsula. On the one hand, they complain that the United States is too intimately involved in Korean matters, arguing that America should leave South Korea to run its own affairs; that, in fact, America's influence in Korea is largely harmful to the true interests of the Korean people. On the other hand, they also complain that the United States has not in the past, and does not still, do enough to promote their own political positions. Thus, for example, they blame the crushing of the Kwangju uprising of 1980 on the Americans and argue that major opposition figures should be championed by the United States against the existing government of the South.

In a phrase, these people want to have their cake and eat it too. American influence, they argue in effect, is bad not in itself, but because it does not support them. They try to capitalize on nationalistic sentiments that assert independence, while at the same time calling for greater American support in their own struggle against the entrenched powers. The democratic ideology shared by America and the Korean opposition frequently leads its adherents into this sort of dilemma.

North–South divide

Another powerful force in the shaping of South Korea is the division of the peninsula into two hostile states at the end of the Second World War and the ideological war that followed this division. The immense material and human destruction suffered by Korea as a result of the latter war colors everything both sides do, and remains a focus of attention and concern even though the South, at least, has become a more populous and powerful economic state than a united Korea had ever been. Virtually every member of the political, industrial, military, commercial, educational and financial elite of Korea can remember the Korean War in vivid, personal terms.

What makes the division of Korea such a significant internal factor – more important than the similar divisions of Germany and Vietnam, for instance – is that Koreans, both northern and southern, see themselves as a single people artificially separated after hundreds of years by forces beyond their control. The Germany which was divided after the Second World War had been a unified nation for less than a hundred years, the divided Vietnam for even fewer years. Both these other countries have large linguistic and ethnic minorities that lessen the degree of uniformity within the national boundaries.

In the minds of most Koreans, however, their divided country is a single nation with a single people and a single language. They lack the ethnic mix of Vietnam and Germany and the geographical–religious split of the Germans. The language, art, dress and social customs of the North are hard to distinguish from those of the South. After over 30 years, most Koreans cannot accept the validity of the division, even if they also cannot offer any practical solutions to the problem of reunification.

Paradoxically, the division of families by the Korean War perpetuates this feeling of unity. Probably ten million people living in the two Koreas are directly affected by these forced separations. Lost members characterize the majority of extended families on both sides of the Demilitarized Zone (DMZ) that delimits North from South. Such a high percentage of the population is involved in this particular problem that the shifting of a few boundaries or the relocation of several thousands of people would provide no solution. This is not just a matter of nationalism or emotions or even Cold War politics; the division of Korea has an immediate, daily impact on a great many families.

Disruption of families as a result of the Korean War was so extensive that even within South Korea alone, families have remained separated for years. The nature of the fighting in the war – with armies sweeping up and down the peninsula several times – left native northerners far in the south and native southerners far in the north, and scrambled up the rest of the population so that reuniting became very difficult. As recently as 1983, South Korean government-sponsored, nationwide television programs reunited thousands of families within the South only. And in September 1985, the first efforts began to re-establish contacts among family members separated by the North–South border.

Such efforts virtually guarantee that reunification will remain a vital topic in Korean politics for some years to come. Despite the fact that the two countries have vastly differing economic, judicial and political systems, despite the years of hostile propaganda and even physical attacks by each side on the other, despite the close involvement of the great powers in the issue, the personal and family elements of the reunification problem in Korea give it an immediacy which belies the obstacles.

Most South Koreans, when asked about it directly,

will first emphasize the barriers to reunification, which are indeed formidable. But having paid due respect to the apparent realities of contemporary world and Korean politics, these same people will express their own personal and heartfelt conviction that the two Koreas should and must be reunited. The majority of politically acute southerners remain hostile to the communism of the North, suspicious of the motives of the northerners, and fearful of forced reunification as a result of military conquest, but they are nonetheless partisans of a single Korea.

Regionalism Having said all the above about the conviction of the vast majority of Koreans that their split country is a single nation, a second, and contradictory, factor must also be emphasized: the powerful regionalism of South Korea. This apparent paradox is simply one of the things which foreigners have to accept about the country, and it might best be understood as similar to the squabbles that take place within a family. Disputes between brothers and sisters, parents and children or husbands and wives can be very harsh even within families that stand strongly united against outsiders.

For thousands of years, Korea was an agrarian society in which very localized regional self-sufficiency and poor transportation systems insured strong local identification. Some areas of the country were relatively rich and powerful, others were poor and less influential. Thus the provinces of North and South Cholla, on the southwest coast, just to cite one example, were generally considered backward and more primitive than the areas around Seoul, Pusan and Taegu, and the standard characteristics assigned by the sophisticated to the less advanced – dirty, dumb, crude, untrustworthy, etc. – came to be attached to people from the Chollas by the rest of Korea.

During the Yi dynasty period (fourteenth–twentieth centuries), a tendency to look down upon people from the Chollas was strengthened by the practice of sending dynastic opponents into exile there as punishment for political and other transgres-

sions. The view of Cholla people as country bump-
kins was then expanded to include notions of political
unreliability, and in fact the·Chollas remain a center
of political opposition in present-day Korea.

Other regional prejudices survive in Korea also.
People from Seoul – that is, those who can claim roots
in Seoul and the surrounding area – are particularly
proud of the advanced, modern nature of their city.
They often consider themselves superior to people
from other parts of the country, a feeling that is
probably a worldwide capital city syndrome. Taegu
people are also especially proud of the fact that a
disproportionate part of the national political and
military leadership comes from their area.

Had Korea remained an agrarian society with a
relatively stable population, regional affiliations
would not have taken on the extraordinary importance that they now have in South Korea, because the
population has been scrambled not only by the
Korean War but also by the massive population shifts
to the cities of the last three decades. Urbanization
has moved thousands of families away from their
traditional native places as the countryside has
emptied itself into the cities. In fact, few countries in
history have experienced such rapid urbanization as
South Korea, where in 1962 almost 70 per cent of the
population lived in rural areas, but in the mid-1980s
the figure was less than 25 per cent.

As befits a people strongly influenced by the
Confucian tradition, Koreans identify strongly with
the place of birth of their ancestors, even when
descendants may be born elsewhere. Thus people
who live in Seoul, for instance, and whose children
were born in Seoul, and who themselves may have
been born in Seoul, may still call themselves 'Cholla
people'; they still identify with their native places.
This means that traditional regional prejudices and
hostilities continue to play a significant role in
contemporary Korean politics long after the physical
origins of these feelings have ceased to be important.

Making sense of the sometimes vituperative attacks
made on one another by political opponents in South
Korea becomes easier with an understanding of the

regionalism that influences so many of the disputes. Cholla people feel that they have long been discriminated against by governments dominated by people from Taegu and the surrounding area. Most of the political opposition feels that Seoul and its environs have too much influence in general Korean developments. Other less prominent regional prejudices also come into play in daily political activities.

Shared goals of an economically and militarily strong Korea with a responsive, representative government sometimes are submerged by disputes based on ancient regional conflicts. Outside observers, and even many Koreans themselves, occasionally lose hope in the promise of a united, stable South Korea with such a government because of the strength of regionalism. But the country is moving to maturity as the rural traditions fade into the past and the realities of a modern, industrialized, urbanized society begin to assert themselves.

Language   Most westerners coming to Korea for the first time are struck by the formality of social relations and the complicated structure of the social order. Both of these things are shaped and reinforced by the nature of the Korean language, and even if a visitor does not intend to learn it well enough to get by in Korea – and relatively few westerners do, since it is an extremely difficult language – some knowledge of the way in which the language reflects and forms the social order will help newcomers to understand what is going on around them.

As used in South Korea today, Korean has three common forms of address – formal polite, informal polite, and informal – and two more rarely used forms. The forms are primarily indicated by the specific verb endings used, and choice of verb ending depends on the perceived relationship between or among the people speaking. Status is conferred in Korea by sex (males being higher in status than females), age (the elder being higher in status than the younger), education (those with doctorates ranking highest, but the specific university or college attended is also taken into account), position or profession (high-ranking military and government leaders have high status, manual workers have low), wealth and finally relationships (family, professional and educational; the relationship between a teacher and his or her students is a very important one).

Choosing the proper form of address is quite important to Koreans, since to use a form the listeners consider too low would be insulting to them and using too high a form would be considered pandering on the part of the speaker. Thus when Koreans meet for the first time, it is important that their status be made clear by the person introducing them or by the exchange of cards containing the necessary information. Otherwise newly introduced Koreans are sometimes reluctant to speak to one another.

There is a movement afoot, especially among university students and young intellectuals, to abandon the forms of address which reflect status. These people argue that the use of forms of address which indicate differences in status is not consistent with the democratic and theoretically classless nature of modern South Korea. Recognizing the power of language to mold the world in which they live, proponents of this change hope that if everyone uses only the formal polite, the cause of equality will be promoted. Given the radical changes that have occurred in Korean society in the last 40 years, it seems that time is on the side of these reformers, although they have made little progress so far.

Speaking Korean

Fortunately for foreigners visiting Korea, no proficiency in the language is expected, although a little effort is greatly appreciated. Learning a few phrases in the informal polite is more than adequate for the short-term or casual visitor: the standard greeting is *ahn-yang-hah-sayo*; 'thank you' is *kahm-sah-ham-ni-dah*. When addressing someone of clearly higher status, or to express high regard, the greeting becomes *ahn-yang-hah-shim-ni-kah*.

Unfortunately, Korean is a very difficult language for westerners to pronounce accurately. One reason for this is that it is an unstressed language; it is pronounced without the normal rising and falling tones of English, German, French, Spanish, and all other Romance and Germanic languages, to say nothing of tonal languages like Chinese and Thai. Only with long practice and intense concentration can most non-native speakers of the language learn to say Korean sentences without the normal stresses of their native tongue.

Translitera-
tion

A second obstacle is posed by the difficulty of transliterating Korean from either its Chinese character or Korean alphabet (Hangul) forms into the Latin alphabet used by most western languages. Korean has common sounds (an unaspirated 'p', for example) that cannot be effectively rendered by specific Latin letters. Depending upon who is speaking and who is listening, the same letter from Hangul sounds sometimes like a 'p' and sometimes like a 'b', without ever being exactly like either. Similar problems surround 'g' and 'k', 'l' and 'n', and sometimes even 'l' and 'r'.

This problem is compounded by the existence of several systems of transliteration, including an official one used on maps, road signs and the like, which baffles nearly all foreigners. For instance, the southeastern province which sounds to native English speakers like 'Cholla-pukdou' (North Cholla province) is rendered in the official transliteration system as 'Chonra-bugdo'. Only patience, a sharp ear, and a facile tongue will help to overcome these difficulties.

The obstacles are formidable but not insuperable. Perfection in clarity, tone and form is not required of foreigners, and in fact most well-educated Koreans are so proficient in at least one western language, usually English, that visitors are rarely expected to know more than a few polite phrases. Foreigners using Korean expressions will be praised excessively for their command of the language, especially by taxi drivers. This is because the effort, not the result, is what Koreans appreciate. Trying a little Korean is both polite and a very effective way to promote goodwill.

Hangul

Hangul, the phonetic alphabet by which all Korean words can be written, is one of the more amazing inventions of the human intellect. Koreans are sufficiently proud of this development to have a national holiday commemorating the achievement, Hangul Day, 9 October.

Unlike almost all other alphabets, and certainly unique among those used for living languages, Hangul was consciously and systematically developed over a very short period of time (about 20 years). Most alphabets have developed only very gradually, being influenced by a great many factors, but hardly ever responding to purposeful manipulation.

Development of this alphabet was overseen by King Sejong, the fourth ruler of the Yi dynasty, who reigned from 1418 to 1450. Before this time, Korean was written only with Chinese characters, and only a very small educated elite was literate. King Sejong set a group of scholars to work on the task of creating, from whole cloth, a simple alphabet that allowed the spoken language to be rendered phonetically.

The goal was to come up with something that could be learned easily, thus increasing the number of literate people in the country. It was especially intended to allow literacy to expand to the female population who, at the time, were apparently considered incapable of learning Chinese characters.

What these scholars came up with was certainly simple, consisting of only 24 letters. The alphabet has an internal logic and consistency that makes it very easy to learn, so what it lacks in beauty it more than makes up for in utility. Nearly anyone can learn to associate the appropriate sounds with the appropriate characters and thereby learn to read, though not necessarily to understand, Korean in a matter of hours.

Actually it is not quite as simple as this. There are shifts in sounds associated with letters depending on their place in a word. For instance, the two Hangul letters used to represent 'street' will be pronounced 'ro', 'lo', or 'no', depending on what sound immediately precedes them. But these exceptions to strict phonetic correlation of specific letters are both small in number and regular. They do not pose major problems to people trying to learn the language, but they do further complicate the matter of transliteration.

Transliteration remains the big problem. The family name that can be rendered as Pak, Bak or Park, in the Latin alphabet, is only one name in Hangul. The same is true for Yi, Lee and Rhee; they are all spelled the same way in Hangul, and are in fact the same name. Things can also get a little more complicated when it is remembered that the same word in Hangul might have more than one Chinese character equivalent. For example, the Chinese character for the 'han' of Han River is not the same as the character for the 'han' of Hangul. By the way, only the written form is called Hangul; the spoken form is called *hanguk mal*, which literally means 'Han country talk'.

North Korea has completely abandoned Chinese character forms of written Korean words, and only Hangul is used. The South tried a number of years ago to effect the same reform, but after a few years found that many of its young people were illiterate with respect to traditional literature. It is a measure of the strength of traditional values in the South that this project was dropped because of this concern. Modern literature and newspapers are now published using only a minimum of Chinese characters.

Getting there

South Korea is a long way away. From the west coast of the United States, a non-stop scheduled airline flight takes at least 11 hours; from London, Amsterdam, Paris or Frankfurt, flights are at least 17 hours long (one-stop) and can last 28 hours. Even travel from Australia and New Zealand will take a minimum of 12 hours. For all but the most experienced travelers, trips of this length are physically and mentally exhausting, requiring anything from a couple of days to a week of recovery. In the case of journeys from the United States and Europe, these long travel times are made more difficult by the crossing of a great many time zones (at least 14 from the US and 6–9 from Europe).

Visitors to Korea can either plan their trip with sufficient breaks to allow for adjustment or they can gird up their loins and tough it out. For those who have never been to East Asia, and have plenty of time, there are many options for stopovers in new and exciting places. For those with limited time or who are particularly intent upon Korea, the long trip must simply be endured.

Air services

One thing is certain: South Korea can only be reached by air. Although it is a peninsula, not an island nation, Korea cannot be reached via surface transportation; foot travel, trains, cars, buses, trucks and horseback are all impossible. South Korea's only land border is with North Korea, and no scheduled land transport crosses the DMZ as yet. In fact, though regularly scheduled ferry and boat services connect Korea and Japan, the latter can generally only be reached by air, so options are little expanded by going to Japan first.

With the exception of a few flights a week from

South Korean national flag
(illustration by Paula Murray)

Japanese cities to Pusan and Cheju Island, all commercial flights to South Korea land at Kimpo International Airport just outside Seoul. Kimpo is a huge, efficient, modern airport serviced by more than a dozen international airlines in addition to the national carrier, Korean Air. Literally hundreds of flights arrive at and depart from Kimpo each and every day, giving it the same sterile, anonymous character of Hong Kong's Kai Tak airport or Tokyo's Narita.

A variety of direct flights are currently available from Europe (Lufthansa and KLM) and the United States (United and Northwest). In the rush to provide additional services for the Olympics, at least four other airlines – Air Canada, Swiss Air, British Caledonian, and British Airways – are presently negotiating for direct flights to Seoul.

At the moment, far more flights from the West require that connections be made in Tokyo or Hong Kong. Korean Air and the national carriers of many East Asian states – Taiwan's China Airlines, Hong Kong's Cathay Pacific, and JAL – make several flights a day each to Seoul from various parts of the region. It is thus very convenient for western travelers to plan layovers in many places either on the way to or the way from Korea, or both.

Several carriers from more distant parts of East Asia – Singapore, Thailand and the Philippines, for instance – offer attractive fares and hotel packages to encourage travelers to visit these places too. For many coming from the West, such packages make good sense because they reduce costs, provide lay-overs and expand the number of places visited. Of course, they also require more time.

Travelers from the West with less time, but who are still concerned that getting to Korea not be too arduous, would be well advised to make the trip in two phases. First, a long flight to either Hong Kong (from the United Kingdom and Western Europe) or Tokyo (from North America), then a shorter hop to Seoul. Those coming from Australia or New Zealand can also conveniently fly to Hong Kong or Tokyo first. Both Hong Kong and Tokyo are fully modern, convenient cities with an abundance of first-class accommodation and a great many moderately priced hotels. Each place offers its own wonders, with Japan especially rich in things to see and do.

Laying over for two or three days in Hong Kong or Tokyo will provide time to recover from the long flight, and also allow first-time visitors to ease into East Asia. Hong Kong is easy to adjust to, particu-larly for native speakers of English, but Tokyo, too, is not a tremendous shock, except for the expense. Brief stays in either place will probably make it much easier to adjust to Korea, which by comparison is consider-ably more different.

Making the trip to Korea via Hong Kong is especially attractive for those coming from the United Kingdom and much of Western Europe. Largely because two British carriers (British Caledonian and British Airways) and one Hong Kong carrier (Cathay Pacific) vie for the heavily traveled London–Hong Kong route, prices are kept reasonable by intense competition. Cathay Pacific (which has the only non-stop London–Hong Kong flight) and British Caledonian use London's Gatwick airport, while British Airways uses Heathrow.

At least three airlines provide direct service between the United States and South Korea. Northwest Orient (from Los Angeles and Seattle), United (from San Francisco) and Korean Air (from Los Angeles) fly non-stop from the west coast, and Korean Air has a one-stop flight from New York. Prices on these carriers are not as competitive as on the London–Hong Kong routes, but Korean Air does offer some special fares from Los Angeles.

Sleeping on the flight
A word to the wise about Korean Air to and from the United States. There are many Koreans in the United States, and large numbers of Koreans travel between the two countries regularly. These include a great many family members, which means lots of young and very young children. Because of the expense of other classes, most such family groups travel in economy class, so the rear portion of the plane has a surplus of children. Most children, especially those in the two- to eight-year-old range, find it very difficult to keep still and reasonably quiet during a 12- to 14-hour plane trip.

Thus sleeping in the economy section of a Korean Air flight to or from the United States can be very difficult. Young Korean children are not disciplined very effectively under the best of circumstances, but no child in this age range can or should be expected to be silent and still for such a long period. Therefore visitors to Korea who think that sleep on the flight is important, or who find young children especially irritating, should book seats in business class, at least, and first class would be even better. This caution should be especially considered by those travelers who want to arrive in Korea refreshed and ready to tackle business or tourism.

Pacing yourself
Finally, another caution: when planning a trip to Korea, first-time visitors from the West should be careful not to include too many other countries; one going in, another coming out should be the maximum. All the countries of East Asia are strange and fascinating to novices, and trying to do too much in a limited time will dilute and confuse all the different experiences. From the United Kingdom and Western Europe, arriving through Hong Kong and departing

through Japan or Taiwan is a lot, while from North America, arriving through Japan and departing through Taiwan or Hong Kong should suffice. Travelers from Australia or New Zealand would be similarly well served by limiting themselves to one stop each way.

Due to the time and expense involved in a trip to Korea, many travelers are tempted to hit all or most of the high spots of East Asia on the same trip. For some this procedure yields memorable results. But for most people, longer stays in fewer places provide more intense and lasting experiences. Korea is a very different sort of country for westerners. Enjoying it to the fullest requires close attention and receptivity. A new country every two or three days, with a new language, new food and new culture, dulls the senses in a short time.

In 1988, Seoul will host the summer Olympics. Obviously, the Games will attract tens of thousands of people to Korea, and equally obviously, this will strain resources in Seoul and elsewhere. Travel and lodging packages will be offered, but reservations will have to be made early to ensure best choice of accommodation. For people who might not other-wise go to Korea, the Olympics will provide a rare opportunity not only to take in the pageantry and excitement of the Games, but also to see a fascinating country. Good planning, done early, should allow those interested to combine these major events into a once-in-a-lifetime experience. The caveat about not overdoing things on a maiden visit to East Asia should be doubly heeded at the time of the Olympics.

Kimpo

Seoul's international airport will look familiar to anyone who has been in a major airport anywhere else in the world. Kimpo's main building is only a few years old, and it is in the modern fashion of sleek glass and metal that produces acceptable, even if somewhat sterile, buildings. Maintenance on the building is rigorous, and all facilities are clean and orderly. There are usually a sufficient number of passport control and customs people on duty to process expeditiously even large planeloads of people. Nearly all tourists can stay in Korea for up to 15 days without a visa, and most European Community nationals can stay 60 days or longer without one. Visas for other tourists can be obtained at the airport, but should be acquired prior to arrival to facilitate entry into the country.

Korea, like many other East Asian countries, has stringent customs inspections, being particularly concerned with weapons, drugs and pornographic materials. One other particular concern – politically subversive material – is more surprising, but unlikely to be an issue, for most visitors. Materials concerning North Korea, communism or Marxism in general are considered subversive. Usually suspect items will be seized for return upon departure, but sometimes they can create serious problems.

Although in recent years restrictions on photography have been relaxed somewhat, Kimpo is still considered an area of national security interest, and tourists should not take pictures inside the terminal or of any portion of the airfield itself. These prohibitions are enforced by the large number of security and military forces at the airport. In some other airports in the country – ones that are shared civilian–military facilities – in addition to restrictions on photography, the window shades of airplanes must remain closed while the plane is on the ground. The security concerns of the South Korean government should be taken seriously by all visitors.

Kimpo to Seoul   Transportation from the airport (which is about 50 km from the major downtown hotels) is provided in the usual diverse forms, namely, buses, taxis and hire cars. The subway system in Seoul does not service the airport, and neither is there a train service to and from Kimpo.

The cheapest way to get from the airport into the city is on the airport buses that run to various hotels, terminating at the Sheraton Walker Hill, and including the Seoul Plaza. For travelers with limited luggage this is a convenient and reasonably swift mode of transportation. The buses depart from Kimpo every eight to ten minutes from very early in the morning until about 9.30 pm. The fare is less than US$1, which is far less expensive than the other options. Even if the buses do not stop at the specific hotel desired, transferring to a taxi once downtown is easier and cheaper than getting a taxi at Kimpo.

Visitors arriving in Seoul with a great deal of luggage, and those choosing the greater convenience of taxi service, will have no trouble getting a cab at Kimpo. In fact, even before leaving the terminal foreigners are likely to be accosted by taxi drivers offering transportation into town. These drivers operate on the edge of the law since they are not supposed to solicit inside the airport but, for a price, they will help carry bags and escort customers to waiting cabs.

'For a price' is the key phrase here, because the fares such drivers can charge are not regulated; rather they must be negotiated between the cabbie and his customers. These drivers are perfectly willing to take advantage of the new visitor to Korea by offering their services for exorbitant rates. They expect to be bargained down; that's one reason they start so high. So one of the major economic features of Korea – bargaining – can be experienced at the very beginning of a visit. This can be very irritating for an exhausted traveler who has just finished a 12- or 14-hour plane trip, so fortunately there is an alternative.

Outside the Kimpo international terminal (and the domestic terminal as well) there are very orderly and well-marked cab lines. Both the more expensive call cabs and the cheaper regular cabs wait in these lines, accepting customers in queue order. The regular cabs are metered and cost about US$8–12 to most major hotels, depending on how far away they are. The call cabs are also metered, at a higher rate, and they cost about US$14–20 for the same trip. The call cabs are generally newer, more spacious, and probably safer than the regular cabs.

Obviously the cab lines can sometimes be quite long, especially if a great many flights have arrived at about the same time. This is what makes the semi-legal and more expensive services offered inside the terminal a viable alternative for some people. It is quite possible that the Korean government will crack down on the hustlers during the Olympics, while at the same time providing extra transport to and from the airport. But even now getting out of the airport is not difficult, and it should become easier in the next couple of years.

Taking money into Korea

Recent arrivals in Korea will have to have some Korean money, called won (which is designated in print by a capital W preceding the amount). Banks and money changers are strictly regulated by the government and must offer the official exchange rate wherever they may be located. Hotels are allowed to offer less favorable rates, so money should be changed at banks or money changers whenever possible. Unlike some Asian cities, most notably Hong Kong, exchange rates offered at the airport in Seoul are identical to those offered outside the airport. Exchange facilities at Kimpo are open whenever international flights are scheduled to arrive so money may be changed virtually at anytime. Outside the airport, hotels offer exchange services from early morning until late at night; while banks are generally open Monday through Friday from 9.00 am until 6.00 pm and on Saturday from 9.00 am until 12 noon.

Currency and cash instruments (travelers' checks, etc.) up to the equivalent of US$5,000 need not be declared. Reconversion of any declared amount is allowed upon departure as long as amounts over the equivalent of US$100 are accompanied by exchange receipts. There is a considerable US dollar black market in Korea, and currency regulations are an important concern of the government. Visitors would be well advised to adhere to the letter of the regulations and avoid all shady activities. (For further monetary information, see the section concerning money in the chapter about shopping.)

Customs and manners

No area of human behavior is so fraught with difficulties as the realm of the everyday, routine human interaction called manners. Especially when people from places as different as Korea and the West come together, the potential for embarrassing, or even offensive, behavior is great. Fortunately for most visitors to South Korea, its people have generally got used to the behavior of foreigners and have developed a high tolerance for discourtesy.

Those visiting Korea must remember, however, that offense derived from cultural differences cuts both ways. That is, while trying to remain sensitive to the demands of Korean society, one must also keep in mind that it is possible for Koreans to act politely according to their culture, but give offense to others in the process. The guests will, of course, be expected to make the greater concessions, but hosts have obligations in this context also.

One rather trivial but revealing example will make this point clearer. When a westerner is given a gift – say a going away gift – at a party or dinner, it is customary for the recipient to open it, comment on it, and offer profuse public thanks. Korean practice, however, requires quite different behavior. Gifts are received with formal, even solemn thanks, but not opened; they are, in fact, more or less ignored. Only once the recipient returns home or the gathering is over and the guests have gone is the gift opened.

Problems arise, of course, when either the recipient or the givers of the gift are from different countries. If a westerner is being feted by Korean friends or co-workers who have considerable experience with foreigners, the general expectation might be that a gift will be opened at the gathering. On the other hand, a westerner trying to be sensitive to Korean customs might just put off opening a gift until after the party. Similarly, westerners giving a gift to a Korean might feel a bit uncomfortable when their gift is formally received and then put aside.

Clearly it is the interaction of two different sets of expectations that give rise to difficulty. If everyone tries to make adjustments for the customary practice of others, things can get muddled and confusing. Koreans may end up acting like westerners, and westerners like Koreans. There is really nothing to be done about this situation, since no hard and fast rules apply. Flexibility and an awareness of possible problems coupled with a willingness to put up with a certain amount of embarrassment are the best approach.

This chapter points out nine other areas in which short-term visitors to Korea are likely to experience some discomfort. There are, of course, a great many more possibilities than these, but they cannot all be covered here. Those illustrated will give a good idea of the kinds of behavior that need to be considered in order to avoid giving offense.

Bowing and handshaking

Westerners shake hands upon meeting or departing; Asians bow in the same situations, or at least this seems to be a widespread popular conception. Koreans usually confound this distinction by doing both.

There was a time – before this century – when Koreans did bow and did not shake hands. However, during the 40 years of the Japanese occupation, bowing gradually came to be associated with the inferior status of Koreans under the Japanese, thus acquiring offensive connotations. When the Americans – a dedicated handshaking people – arrived in the wake of the Japanese departure, this new form of greeting and saying farewell was welcomed.

The continued presence of a great many Americans since 1945, and the addition of many more westerners from other countries, have served to reinforce handshaking as common behavior in Korea. But cultural traditions like bowing are not so easily changed; they persist as nearly instinctive behavior. Therefore it is now normal for Koreans to bow and shake hands.

Korean bowing is neither as exaggerated nor as formal as Japanese bowing. Usually a simple nod of the head will suffice when the person being acknowledged is a casual or passing acquaintance; this sort of gesture is nearly always accompanied by a handshake. Slightly more significant relationships may involve a dipping of the head and shoulders, again with a handshake included.

A more proper bow, in which a distinct bend of the waist occurs, is reserved for very formal situations or when the status of the participants requires an expression of high regard or respect. High government officials and diplomats might exchange the more formal bow, or former students of a particularly revered teacher might use it as a gesture of respect. Often, in an informal setting, even this bow will be followed by handshaking. Westerners in Korea will probably never be expected to make a proper bow except in the most formal situations.

Korean women are less likely to shake hands in any situation than are Korean men. Male visitors will usually avoid embarrassing Korean women by waiting for the woman to offer her hand; otherwise a very brief bow from head and shoulders is acceptable. Female visitors can freely offer their hands to Korean women in almost any situation, but taking the lead from Korean men might be the safest approach.

Touching

This subject is closely related to the above, of course, and it can be a very complicated matter. The major distinction between the western practices of touching – including handshaking, embracing, touching arms, holding hands, etc. – and the Korean is that both Korean men and women do a lot more of it than do their western counterparts.

One of the most striking things about 12- to 18-year old Korean school girls is the amount of close physical contact they have. Not only do they walk hand-in-hand and arm-in-arm, they also drape themselves over one another in groups of four, five and six. Most remarkable of all is the ability of these girls to walk down the street together while leaning against each other in contact from hip to shoulder.

School girls display the most extreme form of

public physical contact in Korea, but among almost all other sex and age groups touching is far more common than in most western countries. Until a few years ago, however, almost all such contact was intrasexual and intrafamilial. Adolescent boys and girls walking hand-in-hand or arm-in-arm were far more often brothers and sisters than lovers. In recent years, this has changed somewhat, making it difficult to judge what the relationship of a male-female couple is.

For visiting foreigners, however, the significant point about Korea is still that physical contact within the sexes is much more common than between them. Women as well as girls touch one another far more often than is common in the West. The closer the relationship becomes, the more frequent is such contact, and female visitors should be prepared for it once they establish friendships with Korean women. Children of both sexes are also quite commonly touched and caressed by Korean men and women.

While Korean men are not as tactile as Korean women, physical contact among teenaged boys and young men is a good deal more common than it is among these groups in the West and slightly more common among adult males. The tendency to touch among this latter group increases dramatically as men consume more alcohol during an evening's festivities. Otherwise quite reserved and aloof Korean men can get positively cuddly after a few drinks. This is another cultural difference that can cause serious embarrassment or offense if not expected.

On the other hand, it is still extremely uncommon for a Korean man to touch foreign women in any intentional manner, except for handshaking. Such intimacy is so taboo that it simply does not happen very often; western women need have little fear of any molestation in Korea. Western men may occasionally be physically accosted in some of the bawdier areas of prostitution, but even this is an infrequent occurrence.

One custom Koreans have that is hard for foreigners to notice, but which nearly all Koreans pay attention to, is the practice of handing objects to people and receiving things from others with two hands. This practice presumably originated at the time when Koreans wore loose-sleeved robes; the second hand was used to pull back the sleeve to reveal that no hidden weapon would surprise the giver or receiver of objects.

Handing and receiving things

Whatever the origin, the custom is one that is firmly ingrained in older Koreans and those highly conscious of their cultural heritage, but less prevalent among youth. Nonetheless, recognizing and practicing it gives foreign visitors to Korea another means of putting their Korean hosts and friends at ease.

In some cases, this practice can take on an almost ludicrous quality. For instance, if some older Koreans have to stretch an arm out to reach something from a great distance, they may almost unconsciously reach across their bodies with their other hand and touch the extended shoulder, or very high on the extended arm. Or someone with an armload of items may gingerly touch only a wrist or palm of the hand that is giving an item to or receiving something from another person.

Normally, of course, people have both hands free when exchanging things with others. In some cases, both the giver and the receiver may extend the arm with the item and reach over to touch that arm at about mid-forearm. More commonly, items are extended or received with two hands, even small items like a pen or a pencil. Obviously, such a gesture serves no purpose but social custom; it is just polite. Of interest to foreigners is the fact that Koreans are not so free with polite phrases (like 'please' and 'thank you') in these situations, although they will nearly always respond to them.

One variation of this custom occurs while making toasts at a dinner or other formal occasion. Under these circumstances, the glass is always held with two hands, one holding the glass, the other supporting it from below. The glass thus held is moved toward each person involved in the toast and raised and lowered slightly. This, too, is one of the situations in which Koreans may follow the western custom of one-handed toasts, while westerners follow the Korean custom of two-handed toasts. Politeness can be confusing.

Shoes Generally, Koreans take off their shoes when they enter a home, many restaurants, and rooms in Korean-style inns. Nearly all homes and public places where this practice prevails provide pigeonholes into which shoes may be placed. In restaurants where shoes are removed to enter a Korean-style dining room, shoes are left outside the room, and during the meal someone from the restaurant turns them around with the toes pointing away from the room so that guests can simply step into their shoes as they depart. Some such restaurants even polish their guests' shoes during dinner.

This practice should suggest two things to foreigners; don't wear socks with holes in them, and don't wear shoes that are hard to get on and take off. Very often Koreans walk around with the backs of their shoes squashed down under their heels, thus allowing the shoes to be slipped on and off easily. Visitors to Korea who plan to go to traditional Korean restaurants or private homes should perhaps have a pair of moccasin-type shoes that are easy to take off and put on.

Surely this custom is one that continues to make sense. If consideration is given to the sorts of things shod feet step into while out of doors, it seems reasonable to prevent many of these things from being taken into homes and restaurants. Usually places where shoes are removed provide slippers or even more substantial sandals for wear inside the house or restaurant. It certainly is easier to keep carpets and floors clean when everyone treading on them wears only indoor shoes.

Large parties in private homes can sometimes result in a jumble of shoes that is difficult to unscramble.

Occasionally, slightly tipsy guests can depart wearing someone else's shoes. Sometimes Koreans are momentarily baffled when they have to leave a house or room by a door other than the one by which they entered. And an emergency such as a fire alarm can result in a bunch of stocking-footed people standing around outside while their hastily abandoned shoes remain inside. But on the whole, this is a custom that continues to serve a good end.

In large part because of the formal quality of most social relations, Korean guests tend to arrive at and depart from social functions with foreigners in groups. It is not uncommon for guests to linger outside a foreigner's home or a restaurant waiting for other guests to arrive so that all can enter together. Similarly, when one member of a group, usually the senior or highest ranking, decides it is time to depart from a gathering, everyone leaves at once.

Arriving and departing

From a westerner's point of view, this practice has its advantages. Usually parties end at fairly definite times; Korean guests, at least, do not normally stay on to the bitter end. This pattern also avoids the awkwardness of having one guest arrive early, requiring entertainment while final preparations are being

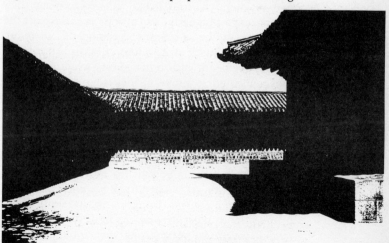

Traditional courtyard
(illustration by Paula Murray)

made. Unfortunately for the novice, all Korean guests tend to arrive a little early.

However, having all the guests arrive together makes it difficult to prepare drinks, take coats and keep shoes straight all at once. Introductions of people who do not know one another can also get complicated when they have to be done *en masse*. Perhaps more difficult for westerners is the rather formal air this practice imposes on almost any gathering. Conversations tend to be general enough to include everyone when it appears that all guests form a single group. The job of loosening up such a tightly knit group can tax even the most experienced host.

This sort of collective action can create hard feelings in westerners if they expect particular Korean friends either to come early or stay late. In the West, quite often good friends of the hosts linger at the end of a gathering for additional, more intimate talk or to help with clearing up. In some cases not doing so can be taken as an affront, or at least as a signal of lack of closeness in a friendship. This is not so with Koreans, who adhere to a more formal set of rules when it comes to such social functions.

If Korean guests behave this way, it provides a clue to foreigners. Korean hosts will expect that their guests arrive a bit early, in a group, and all depart the same way at the same time. Keeping this in mind, westerners should make some effort to coordinate their movements with other guests while not being too concerned to move in lock step. Korean hosts obviously make concessions, and foreign guests should do the same.

Personal relations   Friendships in Korea have a slightly different quality from those in the West, say. Above all else, family relations are most important for nearly all Koreans. Parents, brothers, sisters, aunts, uncles, nieces, nephews and cousins form, in most families, the primary and most frequent social contacts. This tendency remains very strong even though families may have been separated by the move to the cities that characterizes recent Korean history.

After family, school ties are strongest, far stronger than in most western countries. But it is secondary-school ties, not university connections, that are most important, although the latter are very significant as well. In fact, it is safe to say that for the vast majority of middle- and upper-class Koreans, almost all of their social contacts are with family members and fellow schoolmates, either from high school or university. Contacts made professionally or in the work place after leaving school are a distant third as a source of social contacts.

This gives to Korean friendships and social activities a depth of familiarity that strikes foreigners as unusual. Koreans know their friends extremely well because they have known them for a long time, because they have known one another's families well, and because they have closely shared some of the most important events of their developmental years. Such friendships are not unheard of elsewhere, and are not even particularly rare. What makes Koreans different is that practically all of their friendships have this quality.

Beyond immediate classmates, Koreans feel a bond with people who preceded or followed them in the same school by a few years. The mutual obligations of such relations exceed almost any that are felt in western countries, even among graduates of Britain's 'old boy network' or the smaller, more exclusive schools of the Ivy League in the United States. Korea's giant corporations are first of all family affairs and then based on school ties: again, more often than not high-school ties, not university.

School ties apply as much to women as to men, although in Korea's male-dominated society the ties among males are more obvious and more important economically. But both sexes largely define their relationships with non-family members in terms of school acquaintanceships. These ties do not just imply friendship, but also long-term mutual obligations. Schoolmates are supported politically and economically, sometimes even if such support is not in the best interest of the individual giving it. The less reputable and more ambitious can manipulate their friends by playing on the obligations implied by having attended school with someone.

A corollary to these school bonds is the relationship between teachers and their students. Once again, these are relationships that endure long after the school years are over, and they may well link a single individual to more than one former teacher. The student–teacher relationship is one of the central facets of Confucianism, and Koreans quite consciously see the endurance of such ties as evidence that traditional values persevere in their country, providing stability in a changing world.

The pervasiveness and importance of such school-based connections constitute one of the apparently paradoxical features of present-day South Korea. Economically it is a very dynamic country, with businesses rising and falling, areas of development shifting and changing; in terms of geographic mobility, it is an extremely dynamic country, with vast numbers of people having left the countryside for the cities, and with huge numbers moving into Seoul from all over the country. But despite this the traditional social ties, derived from and more suited to an agrarian society with a stable population and a small educated elite, persist in strength.

Children and students
Patterns of child rearing in Korea often strike visitors as most unusual. Until they reach school age, children, especially males, are indulged, pampered and rarely disciplined. Korean parents do not adhere to the adage of 'seen but not heard', and in public places young Korean children can be downright pests. At least westerners often see them in this light; other Koreans for the most part tolerate the sometimes rude and disruptive behavior of children as perfectly normal.

Since Korean children are almost completely excluded from business activities and public entertaining of clients and foreign acquaintances in restaurants, bars, etc., most people visiting the country will not encounter children at close quarters. But in private homes and in public places where children are present – parks, museums, movie houses, and elsewhere – foreign guests will come into contact with small children. Forewarned will be forearmed in this case. Be prepared to have to tolerate fussy, noisy, disruptive and rarely disciplined children.

When Korean children reach school age (five or six), things change dramatically. From the day they enter elementary school until the day they leave high school, Korean children are subjected to rigorous discipline, heavy workloads and close supervision. They are expected to do well in academic subjects as well as music, sports and other extracurricular activities, but the overwhelming emphasis is placed on academic achievement. The Korean educational system is similar to the Japanese in that the basic technique is rote learning, and high scores on national university placement tests depend on memorizing textbooks.

Until a few years ago, entry into a university virtually guaranteed receiving a degree, since no university students failed. Students who had endured the drudgery of 12 years of demanding rote learning had a very strong tendency to let up once they entered a university. Professors and administrators tended to overlook lack of work and achievement in students. Probably one of the reasons Korean university students are famous for protesting and demonstrating is that their studies demanded so little of them, leaving plenty of time for other activities.

In 1981, all this began to change when the government introduced new educational measures that simultaneously expanded the nation's university student population by over 40 per cent (from 250,000 in 1980 to 360,000 in 1981), and decreed that henceforth 30 per cent of all entering freshmen would fail before graduation. This decree set no minimum standards for survival, but simply required that students in the bottom 30 per cent be flunked out, no matter how good their work.

The government apparently sought to achieve two goals with these measures. On the one hand, it hoped to upgrade the level of university scholarship by requiring competition for degrees. The theory was that if students knew that 30 per cent would fail, they would work harder to remain in the 70 per cent that were to survive. On the other hand, the government hoped to be able to use the fear of failing to discipline students who protested and demonstrated against governmental policies. Both goals, if achieved, would reduce the potential of students to be a political force in the country.

University students in Korea have long commanded political influence far out of proportion to their numbers, economic power and access to political decision-making processes. Deriving much of their strength from memories of student-led anti-Japanese protests during the early years of this century, university students have since 1945 brought down one government (Syngman Rhee's in 1960) and created major problems for many others. Students are generally accepted as the conscience of the nation and the hope for the future. This gives them considerable prestige and burdens them with obligations that have little to do with their pursuit of scholarship.

Students led the growing protests against the government of Park Chung Hee in the late seventies; they started the demonstrations that led to the uprising in the southwestern city of Kwangju in 1980; and they conducted the occupation of the United States Information Service library in Seoul in 1985. In between these major events, students kept up an almost endless string of protests and demonstrations. The educational decrees of 1981 have apparently changed little, and in fact most of the more onerous elements have been relaxed. Beginning in 1985, universities have more local autonomy in deciding who passes and who fails, the mandatory 30 per cent fail rate having been dropped.

At the same time that the government began to ease up on some aspects of university regulation, however, it cracked down on others. Police spies, who had been removed from campuses in the early eighties, have returned; student demonstrators, and university administrators who tolerate them, are being summarily dismissed. Students continue to be a major problem for the government, and as long as they are they will continue to have a degree of influence on

Korean politics which far outstrips the influence western students have on their countries' actions.

Gifts and bribes – the distinction between the two being what is acceptable and what is not – pose major problems for foreigners trying to deal with Korea. The so-called 'Koreagate' scandal of several years ago brought some aspects of the problem to the public's attention in the United States, and the continuing struggle for international markets between western and Asian manufacturers keeps the issue alive. On a less exalted level than international relations, understanding Korean customs relating to gifts will make it easier for foreign visitors to enjoy extended stays in the country while dealing with Korean businessmen and public officials. **Gifts and bribes**

Customary practice in Korea requires that, on special occasions, people low on an organizational chart give gifts to those higher up. Gifts are also freely given to people with whom a person or organization has regular or special dealings. In the minds of Koreans, such gifts are tokens of special relationships, not bribes. Their function is to demonstrate goodwill and respect, not to curry favor. While gift giving can be used to insure mutually favorable relationships, it is not intended to be used to buy specific treatment.

The differences between western and Korean views of the function and acceptable limits of gift giving, and when it becomes bribery, are differences of degree, not kind. Bribery is not unheard of in Korea, just as innocent gift giving occurs in the West. But differences of degree are much harder to define than are differences of kind. A complete novice can only rely on the advice and practice of the more experienced: in other words, watch and ask. This is perhaps one realm in which the rather silly guideline of 'if it feels good, do it' applies. Impropriety may take on different limits when westerners deal with Koreans, but subjective responses to specific situations will keep individuals informed on their own behavior.

This chapter ends with yet another observation about the language of Korea and its interaction with social **Saying 'no'**

customs. Koreans think it impolite to say 'no' bluntly
in many situations, such as when dealing with those
perceived as of higher or equal status, when dealing
with foreigners or when any loss of face for either
party will occur. Thus Korea has many ways of
meaning 'no' without saying it, and many ways to
distance a speaker from any action implied by a
statement.

Once again this points up a paradox in Korean
culture. At times Koreans take great pride in being
bold and direct people. Often they will draw unfavorable comparisons between themselves and the
Japanese, whom Koreans often consider to be indirect
to the point of deviousness. Japanese, say Koreans,
always tell listeners what they want to hear, while
Koreans are straightforward and honest even at the
risk of rudeness.

Practice, however, is a different matter. Korean has
a simple word for 'no', *aniyo*, which is frequently
employed in response to direct factual questions: did
you bring an umbrella? Is the library open? Problems
begin when interpretation or judgements are
required: do you think this is a good plan? Are you
enjoying yourself? In answering the latter pair of
examples, Koreans will go to great lengths to avoid a
blunt response of 'no', especially if they perceive the
questioner to be of higher status than themselves.

All languages reflect the cultural realities of the
people who speak them, so Korean has complicated
and convoluted ways to avoid saying 'no'. It does not
provide euphemisms, or – strictly speaking – evasions
or lies, but it does allow ways of suggesting rejection
or objection without stating it. Unfortunately it is not
possible to give an accurate example in English, since
English basically only allows for distortions of
various sorts. Korean, on the other hand, provides for
polite, ambiguous, face-saving ways out of potentially uncomfortable situations.

Foreigners who are not skilled in interpreting such
responses often experience frustration and get
involved in misunderstandings. Negotiations can be
made unnecessarily (as far as foreigners are concerned) complicated by this practice, and time can be

wasted trying to pin down Koreans for a more substantive response. But for Koreans, the process preserves harmony and face, making it easier for positions to change and resolutions to be reached. In these circumstances bluntness limits options, so indirection is preferred. The sooner outsiders make their peace with this fact, the sooner they will be comfortable with and successful in their dealings with Koreans.

Getting around inside Korea's cities

Within cities in Korea there are four major modes of transportation: taxis, cars, buses and going on foot. In addition, Seoul has a subway and Pusan will soon have one. Each mode has its advantages and disadvantages, but some special conditions in Korea make decisions about which mode to use especially important.

Taxis Korean taxi drivers are terrible. They drive too fast, brake too hard and are reckless. An article in *Time* magazine of 3 June 1985, observed that 'Seoul's 35,000 taxicab drivers have the doubtful distinction of being among the world's most dangerous.' This doubtful distinction is the result of many factors, including lack of proper training, unconscionably long work hours, and chaotic traffic conditions.

When an American diplomat and her husband arrived in Korea for the first time some years back, their taxi driver sought to make the trip from Kimpo into the city more pleasant by changing his radio from a Korean language station to the American military station in the country (AFKN, Armed Forces Korea Network), which broadcasts in English. Unfortunately for the somewhat nervous novices, the first item they heard on the radio was a report by the UN on world traffic conditions which identified Korea as having a traffic accident rate that was 30 times the world average and a traffic fatality rate that was 6 times the world average. Fortunately, the newly arrived Americans did not become further additions to these already appalling statistics.

Perhaps the most important reason for the bad record of Korean taxi drivers is that for many years

they have had work schedules that invite disaster.
Although some own their hacks, most taxi drivers
work for companies which require them to be on
duty for as long as 24 hours continuously. Not
surprisingly, after about 18 hours or so even the most
experienced drivers begin to lose some of the sharp
edge of perception and reflexes required to survive
unscathed in the chaos of Korea's city streets. Utterly
bizarre driving behavior can result when a driver
approaches the end of such a demanding day's work.

These long working hours would not be so serious
a problem if they were not coupled with the very low
wages paid to taxi drivers. In order to make a living
wage from their jobs, taxi drivers must squeeze as
many fares as possible into the work day. Most
companies do not operate on a minimum requirement, meaning that each driver must return a
specified amount to the company for each day's work
and gets to keep the surplus for himself. Rather the
companies pay the drivers a straight percentage of
fares received, and the rate is so low that a maximum
number of fares must be hauled to make the time
spent in the cab worth while.

These two aspects of·taxi service in Korea often
give rise to unusual situations. Since the taxi companies do not normally provide central rest facilities
for their employees, drivers must grab food, beverage
and toilet time when and where they can. Foreign
travelers in Korea are sometimes surprised to have
their taxi drivers stop in the middle of a trip to find a
place to relieve overstrained bladders and bowels.
Trips often take longer than expected because drivers
have to stop for food or drink, which is often just a
little hot tea drunk from a glass jar and a bit of rice. In
addition to being dangerous, the life of a Korean taxi
driver is not a particularly pleasant one.

However, for the reasonably well-heeled foreigner
there is an option to entrusting one's life to an
over-tired, under-skilled, and economically pressured
cabbie. The situation described above prevails for the
large majority of taxis that can be hailed on the
streets, but not for the much smaller number of call
cabs. These are more expensive, usually in better

repair, and are driven by drivers who are generally better paid and trained, more cautious, and do not work such long hours. These cabs are available at major hotels, most airports or by calling the telephone numbers prominently displayed on the sides of the cabs seen in the streets.

It is, of course, more than likely that short-term visitors to Korea will travel frequently in the standard hail cabs without ever being involved in even a minor accident, let alone a fatal one. But nearly everyone who spends longer than a month or two in major cities is almost certain to experience at least a fender-bender, and the unfortunate may do much worse. While there is no guarantee of safety, call cabs are a better bet than hail cabs, and the daylight hours are safer than the late night hours.

Unless one hires a car, taxi travel is very hard to avoid altogether. Even though Seoul and other large cities have some centrally placed hotels (like the Seoul Plaza, the Chosun and the Lotte in Seoul), offices and tourist sights are usually spread out over a wide area, making traveling fairly long distances a necessity. Furthermore several of the best hotels in Seoul (the Shilla, the Ambassador, and the Sheraton Walker Hill, for instance) are quite a distance from the major attractions, both business and tourist. For many travelers, taxis are the only hope of getting around in a limited time, and reasonable fares make them a viable option.

New fares for hail cabs were introduced in November 1985. A time factor has been imposed on to the old distance rate of US65¢ for the first 2 km and US5¢ for each additional 400 m. A surcharge of US5¢ per one minute and 36 seconds spent traveling at or under 15 km per hour will be added to the final charge. Given the severely crowded streets of Seoul, Pusan and other cities, where gridlock always seems an imminent danger, the new charge will almost certainly cost taxi riders a good deal.

Two special warnings   While bridges across the Han River are numerous and free, Seoul does have a number of toll tunnels, one particularly prominent one being on a favorite taxi route to the airport from downtown. People riding in cabs are expected to pay the toll (about US10¢) at the tunnels, and drivers will frequently turn and ask for the toll while approaching the tunnel at a high rate of speed. The wise traveler will be prepared to hand over the toll in exact change quickly, so as to reduce the danger of a driver not watching the road. Some drivers will pay the toll themselves and then add the amount of the toll to the final fare.

Korean taxi drivers, especially those outside Seoul, have another habit which is noted by almost all foreign visitors: they honk their horns nearly incessantly. Seoul has strictly enforced laws to limit the use of horns, but other cities are rather more lax about enforcement. Provincial cities like Kwangju in the southwest and Taejon in the center of the country fairly ring with the horns of taxis. More often than not, taxi drivers are merely announcing their presence to potential customers rather than warning of potential danger.

Hire and rental cars

Hire cars, which come with a driver, have long been available in Korea, and although they are expensive, for visitors strapped for time they are the best choice. Most travel agencies and all major hotels can provide help with arrangements. Generally the cars are large, well cared for and driven with competence and courtesy. Nearly all Koreans with enough money employ full-time drivers, so this mode of transportation is not just acceptable, but expected of people the Koreans perceive to be of high status. Using a hire car to move around the city while conducting business or professional negotiations can assist in establishing rapport and acceptance.

One of the common sights around Korea that first-time visitors often comment on is the large numbers of men seen standing around parked cars. Sometimes these men are vigorously washing or polishing the cars, but usually they are simply wiping them, talking with one another and having a smoke. The amount of time and energy that goes into keeping cars clean in Korea is a measure of the state of economic development and income distribution, since only the very wealthy can afford the luxury of a full-time driver. Many of the drivers are provided by companies, as are the cars, and many others are family members of the car owners.

Late in 1984 Korea began its first experiment with rental cars when Hertz opened offices in Seoul (at the Lotte and Shilla hotels) and the southern resort island of Cheju; Avis has since added an office at the Lotte also. Both Hertz locations have very limited resources (200 cars in Seoul in mid-1985 and 30 in Cheju). Those who want to drive themselves must be at least 25 years old and present a valid passport and an international driver's license when renting a car.

However, except for the most adventurous of travelers, a self-drive rental car is not a viable option. City driving in Korea is extremely difficult and hazardous, streets are poorly marked, and direction signs are usually in Hangul. At rush hours in the morning and evening, traffic is extraordinarily heavy, and in Seoul and Pusan traffic is heavy all day long. City streets are rarely laid out in grid fashion, intersections frequently are the conjunction of five or six streets, and one-way streets and U-turn regulations make it very easy to get lost even when in sight of one's destination.

Nevertheless, both rental cars and hire cars offer an advantage for the short-term visitor that is well worth considering, namely the freedom to roam about the countryside of Korea. Trains, and especially buses, travel through the countryside, but only on specific routes and schedules. A rental car or a hire car with driver allows visitors to break away from the fixed routes and schedules to investigate and explore. As the major cities of Korea become more and more standardized and sterilized by modernization, the countryside becomes increasingly attractive for the glimpses of traditional Korea it can offer.

Highway driving

In rather sharp contrast to city driving in Korea, highway driving is quite pleasant. Korea has a superior network of super highways which connect most of the major cities. The roads are very well constructed, have excellent drainage, and are passable in all but the coldest, snowiest periods. Even at the latter times, the major highways are quickly cleared, for much commerce passes along them.

Major roads are well marked and well lighted. Road signs are generally transliterated, and some are even in English. The road surfaces and verges are kept tidy and free of obstructions; and they are frequently patrolled by police and highway service vehicles. Service areas and rest stops with toilet and food facilities are conveniently located, clean and open long hours.

Once foreign drivers get on to these roads, it is easy for them to travel from city to city. Korean drivers are, for the most part, quite adept at driving on super highways. Most drive in the right-hand lane except when passing, and lane changes are almost always signaled. Since Korea has very strict inspection and licensing laws, both cars and drivers are usually in good condition.

Korean drivers have one very disconcerting habit when driving on highways: they do not turn on their headlights until it is really dark. Thus, as the sun begins to go down, visibility gets to be a big problem. On-coming traffic is hard to see, making passing on and crossing two-lane roads hazardous. Given all the other safety-conscious practices and laws of Korean driving, this custom is puzzling to foreigners, and those who plan to drive at night must be doubly cautious during the transition period from light to dark.

Trucks can also be a problem on the major highways, not because they are badly driven but simply because there are so many of them. Although the highways are generally laid out to avoid steep terrain, the country is so mountainous that almost all roads have an abundance of hills, some of which are quite formidable. Large diesel trucks cannot maintain their speed on such inclines, and this, combined with their number, can cause significant slow downs in a great many places.

Especially on the Seoul–Pusan expressway, a large part of the truck traffic consists of small- to medium- *Special peculiarities* sized vehicles carting the household effects of families making the move to Seoul. As one approaches the capital city, the number of these trucks increases rapidly. Probably nothing that foreigners can observe directly gives such a powerful sense of the flow of South Korea's population into Seoul. People might not be voting for modernization with their feet, but they are with their household goods.

Periodically along Korean roadways there are widenings, half a mile or more in length; the number of lanes in the road does not increase, the road just widens considerably. These are intended to serve as emergency landing strips in case of war. The Korean military, having experienced the Korean War, is highly conscious of the extent to which modern warfare is dependent upon air transport; it also is aware of how vulnerable to attack from the North its major airfields are. To guard against a loss of landing strips, these wide spots have been built into most highways and a great many secondary roads also. So far they have not been put to use, except for training and drills; with luck, they will never be used as intended.

In the meantime, they are put to another use which creates a potential traffic hazard that all drivers in the country should be aware of. During harvest time, these wide spots in roads are used to dry grain: rice, barley, millet and others. In some cases, as with millet, the grain is spread across the road so that vehicles can pass over it, thus separating the grain from the husk.

More commonly, rice is spread out in a thin layer along the road side to dry. It is periodically raked and swept so that it dries thoroughly, then it is sacked up, weighed, and sold. Dry grain stores better than moist, which is why this procedure is followed. However, during harvest time, drivers must be especially cautious not to run down the people working the grain, who usually are children and older men and women.

In case of an accident   Foreingers driving in Korea, as well as passengers in taxis for that matter, should be well aware of the

customs and regulations surrounding traffic accidents. The first rule is to leave the vehicles where they
are after an accident: don't move them out of the line
of traffic or to unblock passageways, however sensi-
ble and prudent such actions may seem. In Korea
vehicles are left in place until the police arrive.
Obviously, drivers and even passengers of vehicles
involved in accidents should not leave the scene until
the police arrive, unless medical care is an urgent
necessity.

Foreigners who do not speak Korean will have to
rely on Koreans to notify police and emergency
services in the case of an accident. In major cities this
will pose no problem because policemen are everywhere, and accidents immediately draw crowds. In
the countryside, lack of language skills may form a
serious obstacle, but here too any Koreans involved
in an accident can be relied upon to notify the
authorities. Major highways in South Korea have
emergency telephone boxes distributed along them,
and the people receiving calls on this system can
usually understand enough English to grasp the
essence of an emergency; as noted earlier, these
highways are also regularly patrolled by police cars.

Establishing responsibility in an accident is of
paramount importance, and most commonly all
parties involved are held responsible to some extent.
Visitors to Korea who have experience with other
Asian countries will be familiar with this point of
view. As an old Asia hand once described the system,
all parties are automatically 10 per cent responsible by
virtue of having been born into this world. From
there on, responsibility is doled out according to the
extent to which law and custom have been broken. In
quite a literal sense, there is no such thing as an
accident in Korea; somebody, usually everybody, is
responsible to a certain degree.

Buses

All of Korea's major cities have abundant bus
services, and most workers travel to and from their
work places by bus. Students are also heavy users of
buses, as are, of course, other people who need to get
around. Travel by bus is the cheapest form of

transportation except for walking (US27¢ for cash payment; tokens available from small booths near major stops are US25¢), and a great many people use the city bus systems.

Despite the phenomenal number of buses in a city like Seoul – it is common during the rush hours to see 30 or more buses moving down the main streets one after the other – most buses are extraordinarily crowded in the morning and evenings. People are often crammed into a bus in such numbers that some passengers are literally lifted off the floor. Little old ladies with heavy packages and students with large book bags take their toll on other people's knees under these conditions.

If only because it is the most popular form of transportation, visitors to Korea should try riding on a bus in a city at least once. Buses are clearly marked by numbers corresponding to their routings, and guides to routes are available at various places. Those unfamiliar with the city in which they are traveling will, of course, have difficulty recognizing stops, but a written note from hotel desk personnel or a Korean friend will get results when shown to nearly anyone on a bus. Korean buses have attendants, mostly young girls, who help people on and off, and they are usually willing to help the confused foreigner to the best of their ability.

During the non-rush hours, bus riding can be a pleasant and informative way to learn about Korea's major cities. Buses generally go where people want to be, and riding there with them gives visitors an opportunity to find out where and how most people live. Exercising caution about being trapped somewhere that will require travel during the rush hours is prudent, but even that experience is memorable, though hardly pleasant. The density of human population in Korea is never quite so evident as when traveling on an extremely crowded city bus.

Waiting for buses In an effort to clear up special problems in Seoul before the Olympics in 1988, the government has launched a major campaign to get people to stand in orderly lines to board buses. Prior to this campaign, the swiftest and those with the sharpest elbows boarded the buses first without regard to queue or priority of waiting time. The campaign has been reasonably successful to date, and should establish order eventually.

Especially in the larger cities, major stops are used by buses on many different routes, but the buses of a particular route have no designated stopping place at these large stops. If no other bus is at the stop when one arrives, the driver simply pulls in at the front; if other buses are at the stop, the driver pulls in behind them. Since especially busy stops may serve eight or ten different bus routes, this can lead to major discrepancies between the location of an orderly queue waiting for a particular bus and the place that bus stops.

This somewhat random approach frequently leads to chaos, since potential riders can never be certain where their bus will stop. The arrival of a popular bus often results in panic as riders guessing that the bus will stop toward the front of the queue rush to catch it when it stops at the back, or vice versa. The introduction of specific line-up spots should gradually sort out this bit of chaos.

Walking around in the big cities of Korea is, **Walking** unfortunately, rather difficult. Sidewalks are crowded, pavements often uneven, and on the smaller streets pedestrian and vehicular space is not always clearly defined. On the other hand, walking gives the closest, most intimate view of what is going on, and in many of the busiest areas, pedestrian subways and overpasses make it easy enough to avoid the heavy surface traffic.

Seoul in particular has pedestrian subways under nearly all intersections in the heart of town. Originally designed to serve as air-raid shelters as well as pedestrian walkways, these structures are frequently lined with shops. Some of the most interesting shopping areas in Seoul are underground, and several of the major hotels take advantage of this by placing their own shops at the same level.

Whether in the pedestrian subways or on the

surface, though, walking on the busy streets of
Korea's major cities is not for the faint of spirit. The
crowds are always heavy and always rushing, and
manners are not always uppermost in the minds of
those striding purposefully from one place to
another. Being bumped about by fellow pedestrians is
to be expected; Koreans apparently do not notice the
buffeting they both give and receive.

Murmured apologies and giving way to someone
else are rare occurrences, but this should not be
interpreted as lack of manners. The rule of the street
in Korea is that one looks out for oneself. Koreans
themselves sometimes explain that their country is
too small and too crowded for the niceties of courtesy
and concession to others while walking the sidewalks.
The congestion and vigor of large city populations
naturally give rise to a bit of roughness.

In fact, walking the busy streets of Seoul highlights
another of the many paradoxes of South Korea. On
the one hand, it is a very formal and polite society, as
befits a culture strongly and proudly influenced by a
Confucian ethic. Official functions, personal meetings, meals and even informal conversations are
marked by an attention to forms and protocol that is
surprising to most visitors, and even upsetting to
many. Americans and Australians, especially, are
more comfortable with casual, unstructured situations, and are often put on edge by the emphasis given
by Koreans to highly formalized behavior.

On the other hand, in crowded buses, offices and
and stores, on busy sidewalks and in a great many
public places, Koreans seem, if not rude, then little
concerned with the small gestures that make such
situations less unpleasant. This difference between
public and private behavior is striking to all who
come in from outside, but it is little remarked upon or
noticed by Koreans themselves. It is an important
cultural difference between westerners and Koreans
that should be kept in mind by visitors. The tendency
to take offence when confronted by apparently rude
behavior can be tempered by an understanding of the
intention of the actors

Walking around the streets of large cities can give

visitors a more intimate view of what goes on, but some Korean customs limit how much can actually be seen, especially in residential areas. Most Koreans live in large high-rise apartments or in houses that are surrounded by high walls which block off all views from outside. This is another example of the private–public distinction in Korean culture and strongly reflects the family-centered orientation of Koreans.

However, in older residential sections, there is still a relatively busy street life, especially during the summer and early fall months. In many neighborhoods, an active peddlers' trade is still conducted, and observing the practices of the sellers and the buyers can be quite interesting. One striking feature of these peddlers is the distinctive sounds used to announce their presence. Bean curd peddlers in Korea announce themselves by ringing large hand-held bells, while trash metal collectors clack heavy metal-cutting scissors. These are things which cannot be experienced except by living in particular neighborhoods or strolling through their streets at the proper times.

Seoul residential rooftops
(illustration by Paula Murray)

Subways   Seoul was the first South Korean city to get a subway system, followed by Pusan. Seoul's recently completed lines three and four give that city the sixth longest subway complex in the world, and planned expansion will make subways even more important in the future as Korea's cities continue to grow. Especially in Seoul, city planners hope that a good subway system will help relieve the congestion of the surface streets as the city expands south of the Han River.

Except for very heavy crowding during the morning and evening rush hours, Seoul's subways are quite nice. Bright, clean, well-maintained cars and stations with an abundance of route maps in a clear, color-coded system make it easy for foreigners to get the hang of the subway lines. In the downtown area, stations are strategically placed to make access from the major hotels simple.

Again in preparation for the Olympics, the national and the Seoul city governments have gone to great lengths to ease the way for foreign visitors to use the subway. Station names and instructions are available in transliteration and in English at the major stops. Maps on the walls have prices clearly indicated, and booth attendants are willing to make an effort to help out when not harried by the press of rush hour. Given the often remarkable congestion of Seoul's surface streets, the wise traveler will do as much moving about the city as possible by subway.

The completion of the Seoul system in the fall of 1985 led to a reform of the fare structure. The city is now divided into two zones, inner and outer; the fare within a zone or across one zone boundary is US40¢, crossing two zone boundaries will cost US60¢. From most of the major hotels, it will cost US40¢ to travel to the main Olympic venues at the Seoul Sports Complex and the National Sports Complex

Traveling within Korea's major cities is very like traveling within major cities anywhere else in the world. The taxi situation makes things a little different, as does the nature of residential areas. What might surprise first-time visitors to Korea is the extremely busy, almost hectic quality of the streets of Seoul, Pusan and other large cities. The economic miracle in South Korea has, unfortunately, created the same conditions that make the streets of Tokyo, Rome, Taipei and New York so noisy, dirty and crowded.

For some, Koreans and foreigners alike, this pace of life is a definite drawback; for others, it is simply proof of the dynamic growth of the society. The problems of Seoul have been particularly difficult to solve because of the city's enormous size and importance, but the public transportation systems there match those of nearly any other large modern city. Once the subway system has been completed, Seoul will be no more difficult to travel in than are Tokyo and New York.

Air-raid drills

One special condition does prevail in Korea, in the cities and the countryside alike. Once a month the nation has air-raid drills. During these, all unofficial traffic must stop, vehicles must pull to the side of the street or road and pedestrians (and vehicle occupants in the cities) must seek shelter in air-raid facilities. Usually these drills are announced beforehand (in the English language newspapers, among other places), and tourists should plan, if possible, to be indoors during them.

Those caught outside should follow the lead of people around them and do it swiftly. There is nothing casual or frivolous about these drills; military and police officials will be on hand to see that shelter requirements are enforced. Virtually the entire nation takes part in these drills, in the cities and the countryside. Tourists, especially in Seoul, can get a chilling sense of the precarious state of peace on the peninsula by participating in these exercises.

What to see, where to stay, how to get there

Korea has no one great thing to see – no pyramids, no Stonehenge, no Great Wall. In a very real sense, the miracle to see in South Korea is the country itself. From the utter devastation of the Korean War, the new and modern South Korea has risen like a phoenix from the ashes. Unfortunately for those seeking the ancient and time honored, much of this was destroyed by the years of war and can never be rebuilt. Even much of the movable treasure of the country – the great Koryo celadon, the wooden furniture of the Yi dynasty and the primitive pottery of the early Shilla period – has been destroyed or taken elsewhere.

Some treasures survived the pillage and destruction to be preserved in the National Museum in Seoul and in provincial branches in Kwangju, Kyongju and other cities. A great many city gates, palaces and temples have been restored, some many times, and the ancient Shilla capital of Kyongju has been largely excavated and reconstructed to form a massive outdoor museum without walls. Beyond this, Korea's government has made significant efforts to preserve dance, drama, music and festivals associated with traditional Korea. These living cultural treasures are also well worth seeing.

However, the country itself, both the natural beauty and the man-made wonders, is what usually impresses visitors. South Korea has nothing to match the sheer massiveness of the Andes, Rockies, or Himalayas, but it does have some of the oldest and most striking mountains in the world. In the spring, the mountains that cover nearly 70 per cent of the country are a mass of wild azaleas; in the fall, they are ablaze with the changing colors of the season. Even the endless tiny plots of rice offer soft, lush, green expanses in the summer. Finally, few images are more impressive to the first-time visitor than the sight of bright orange persimmons on trees bare of all foliage against a background of new fallen snow in winter.

At least four things in Korea come into the 'must see' category; seeing them all will give first-time visitors a satisfying taste of what Korea has to offer, and should also tempt visitors to stay longer or return again for a fuller meal of the country's delights.

As one of the ten largest cities in the world, Seoul would be worth seeing even if most travelers didn't have to arrive there anyway. No other place in the country captures the miracle of Korea's recovery and growth as well as its capital city. Those familiar with Seoul during the Korean War would have a hard time believing it is the same place if they were to return now for the first time. **Seoul**

Traditionalists bemoan the fact that Seoul looks like most other modern Asian cities: Tokyo, Hong Kong, or Singapore. These same people recommend the countryside, or at least far smaller cities, for a taste of the 'real' Korea. But what could be more real than the city in which more than one-quarter of the national population lives and to which over 100,000 people move every year? Seoul is the Korea of the present and the future, and it is a city that works fairly well, given its size, growth rate and population density.

The vigor, disorder, huge buildings and endless activity are the major things to see in Seoul. On the streets of downtown, the millions of Seoulites can be seen rushing, working, buying and selling every work day. The traffic is at the same time deplorable and amazing. The modern stores, banks, hotels and restaurants are monuments to the nation's vitality: some are beautiful, some are sterile, but all are very real.

In addition to soaking up the character of Seoul itself, the National Museum and the National Folklore Museum in the grounds of Kyongbok Palace should be seen for their displays of the best of both high and popular culture in Korea's past. Not far outside the city, the Korean Folk Village demonstrates many aspects of traditional rural life in living form. More formal traditional culture can be enjoyed at Korea House, which serves buffet lunches and dinners featuring many different kinds of Korean food, and offers evening dance programs with both folk and court dances performed.

Both the Folk Village and Korea House are sponsored by the Korean government, and both are highly artificial, but sincere, efforts to preserve some of Korea's past. Most of these things exist now only as relics and will survive only as long as government subsidies and tourists support them. They exemplify the dilemma Korea, and other developing countries, find themselves in: how to modernize without destroying national uniqueness. The Village and the House are part of the answer, and both are very well done. Nonetheless, one leaves them with the feeling that even this best of possible answers is not good enough.

Haein-sa Located about one-and-a-half hours outside Korea's third largest city, Taegu, Haein-sa ('sa' is a suffix meaning temple) is not the largest, oldest or most beautiful temple in the country, but it probably is the only one that should not be missed. It has nearly everything the other major temples have: a terraced landscape set in a rugged terrain, a large number of rebuilt and well-maintained shrines, hermitages and minor temples, and resident monks who make it a working Buddhist temple. The streams that cascade through the grounds and the beautiful deciduous trees make Haein-sa especially attractive in the fall.

What sets Haein-sa apart from the dozens of temples in Korea that are as or more beautiful is that it is the repository of the so-called Tripitaka Koreana; this makes the temple worth a special trip. The Tripitaka is truly one of the most remarkable tributes to human faith and diligence to be found anywhere in the world.

The Tripitaka is a set of more than 81,000 large, hand-carved, wooden printing blocks, representing the most complete compilation of Buddhist religious teachings in Asia. Carved in the first half of the thirteenth century, most of the blocks are today still in good enough condition to be used for printing. They are stored in cleverly designed, well-ventilated buildings to prevent rot, and they have been guarded by Buddhist monks for more than six centuries. Though most of the temple buildings have been destroyed and rebuilt, the blocks themselves have survived relatively intact.

Librarians of the world have to be astounded by this achievement, and archeologists can only wonder at the feat. The creation of the blocks – by royal order during a Mongol invasion to entreat the Buddha's protection of the Korean people – was miracle enough, marking as it does an amazing melding of intellectual skills and manual labor. But their preservation and survival in a country racked with wars across the centuries and with bitterly cold, dry winters and hot, humid summers, are dumbfounding feats. Chance has to have been a factor, of course, but human wit and dedication are mainly responsible for this marvel.

Visitors to Korea who miss Haein-sa will miss the closest thing to a wonder of the world that Korea has to offer. Contemplating the achievement in the abstract and then viewing it in person offers a true thrill to those who may sometimes despair of the human condition. If humans can do this across a period of 600 years, they can also figure out how to last another 600 or 6,000 years. It is inspiring even for the unbeliever.

Sorak-san

Mount Sorak ('*san*' is a suffix indicating mountain) is one of the highest peaks in South Korea at 1,550 m; it is located in the midst of the area called the Switzerland of Korea. Sorak-san means 'Snow Peak Mountain', and it does indeed have snow on its peak for much of the year. The natural beauty of the area is its major attraction: rugged mountains, hiking trails, and clear, fresh air.

Mountains are a major feature of Korea's terrain; they can be seen from everywhere in the country.

Although even the highest of them cannot begin to match the great peaks of Tibet, the western United States and the Alps, most of Korea's mountains are very old. They have an aged, rugged quality that makes them seem higher than they are, but they rarely evoke feelings of serenity in viewers.

Unfortunately for ski buffs, the rugged nature of Korea's mountains makes them unsuitable for skiing. There is one ski area near Sorak-san – the Dragon Valley ski resort, 24 km south – but when it has snow, it is usually extremely crowded. Winters in Korea's mountains can be very severe, but the natural beauty of the peaks and valleys is enhanced by snowfall. Go for the beauty and the hiking, but not for the skiing.

The major mountain regions of Korea, especially Sorak-san, are very popular places of escape for the country's vast urban population. This means that except during the worst weather, these places are

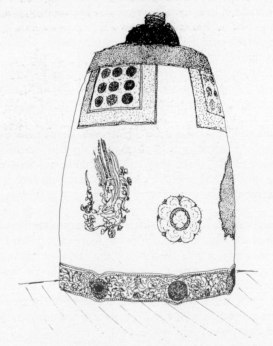

The Emillie bell, Kyongju (height, 3.3m; weight, 205 kg)
(illustration by Paula Murray)

nearly always crowded with Korean and foreign tourists. It is not at all unusual to travel for an hour or more over rough, poorly maintained, unpaved roads to reach a well-known mountain site, only to find that dozens of tour buses have come earlier, disgorging hundreds of Korean tourists.

Nonetheless, the beauty of the mountains is worthy of a visit, and Mount Sorak is among the most beautiful. It is also quite easy to reach from Seoul and has adequate accommodation. The popularity of Sorak-san with Koreans makes it even more interesting, since a visit there will provide insight into what Koreans find attractive about their own country.

One word of warning: Koreans visiting mountains and temples often have picnics at these sites, and the picnics often involve the consumption of large quantities of liquor. A common sight, and sound, at these places is groups of Koreans – quite often all women – dancing and singing in states of mild to extreme inebriation. It is all quite jolly and harmless enough, but Koreans traveling with foreign visitors are likely to be embarrassed by and censorious of such behavior. In a society which is otherwise quite decorous and restrained in 'public, this phenomenon is quite surprising the first time it is encountered.

Kyongju

Last on the 'must-see' list is the ancient Shilla dynasty (57 BC to 935 AD) capital, Kyongju. Designated in 1979 by UNESCO as one of the ten major ancient-city sites in the world, Kyongju was capital of Korea during its 'golden era' in the seventh and eighth centuries AD. In the eighth century, the city had nearly one million inhabitants and was the fourth largest city in the world, after Constantinople, Baghdad and Changan. It was during the Shilla period that Korea was first unified, Buddhism and Confucianism were introduced, and art and high culture first flourished

Much of Kyongju has been excavated, much restored, and much more reconstructed. It is such a treasure trove of ancient pieces that days could be spent in just casual viewing, while two months or more might be required for serious, detailed study of all the displays. With the exception of the Sokkuram Grotto, site of a marvelous collection of sculpture, all of the major locations are open to the public.

Many of the central features of Kyongju are located in the city proper within easy walking distance of one another. Chomsongdae, perhaps the world's oldest observatory; Tumuli Park, site of two large Shilla tombs from which were excavated more than 10,000 items; and the Kyongju National Museum, which includes hundreds of examples of the high artistic skill of the Shilla period, are all in close proximity. A great many other treasures are located a short distance from the city, including Pulguk-sa, probably Korea's most famous and popular temple, about 16 km distant.

Getting there
Since nearly all the things foreigners want to see in Korea are also very popular with Koreans, nearly all of them are easy to get to by bus or bus–train connections. Using Seoul as a departure point, the trip to Kyongju can be made in five hours by bus, to Sorak-san in about six hours by bus to Sokcho (a nearby town) and then a short bus ride to the mountain, and to Haein-sa in four hours by train or bus to Taegu, then 90 minutes by bus to the temple village.

Buses and trains are abundant in Korea. For instance, there are nearly 40 trains each day which connect Seoul and Taegu, and the stations in both cities are near the heart of town. Bus services are even more frequent: one departs Seoul for Taegu every five minutes from 6.00 am until 8.00 pm, but the bus stations are less conveniently located. Whether traveling by bus or train, taxi rides at both ends will generally be necessary.

It is also possible to fly to many cities in Korea, but there are no competing airlines; Korean Air is the only domestic carrier. Flights are infrequent, airports are usually far outside the cities and fares are four to five times higher than those of bus or train. Counting the time it takes to get to and from airports and to wait in various lines at airports, travel by air inside Korea is rarely faster than using buses or trains.

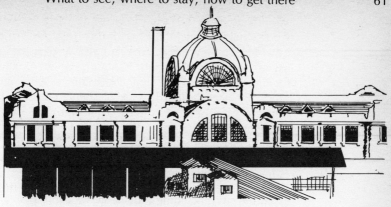

Seoul railway station
(illustration by Paula Murray)

Highway express buses run by at least ten different companies serve nearly all cities of any size. The buses have only one class of service, are generally comfortable, and have in recent years improved considerably on their previously rather weak safety records. Larger cities usually have more than one bus terminal, so travelers should make certain they go to the correct one to start a trip. Advance ticket sales are available and highly recommended in periods during and around holidays and weekends. Fares are very reasonable; travel to even the most distant cities from Seoul, Pusan and Yosu, costs less that US$10.

Train travel is equally good in Korea, but a little more complicated in fare structure and classes of seats and trains. Super express trains, called *Saemaul*, connect Seoul with Pusan, Mokpo, Chonju and Kyongju. There are also express trains (making a few more stops), and local services (making a great many stops). The *Saemaul* trains have several classes of seats and non-smoking cars. All trains are quite comfortable (although sometimes overheated in the winter) and very safe. Lowest fares on local trains for unreserved hard seats are about the same as for buses, and the highest priced *Saemaul* seats are about twice as expensive.

The primary concern of the non-Korean speaking foreigners traveling in the country is making certain they are going to the right place. South Korea has two cities named Kwangju, one five hours from Seoul, the other half an hour outside the capital. It also has cities called Kyongju, Chungju, Chonju, Chongju and Chinju. The potential for confusion is obvious, especially considering the lack of standardization in transliteration of Korean place names into the Latin alphabet. All these places have distinct Hangul and Chinese character names, but their Latin forms can be very confusing. The only way to be safe is to have a Korean acquaintance write down the name of the destination; all hotels will assist foreigners with this service, and many will arrange for the purchase of tickets.

Choosing your mode of transport

Within the country, travel by bus or train is much preferable to travel by air. Furthermore, since one of the most attractive aspects of the country is its natural beauty, airplanes cut out some of the best things to see. Considering safety, cost and convenience, trains are best between major cities; buses on the main routes are nearly as safe and slightly cheaper, and on the back roads and little traveled routes, buses are the only mode available except for the much more expensive taxis.

Actually, for groups of four or fewer people and trips of only a few hours, say from the Taegu train or bus station to Haein-sa, taxis might be a good choice. If foreigners can make themselves understood, and if agreement can be reached on price (writing down figures in order to be certain there is no misunderstanding is usually a good idea), a taxi driver willing to undertake such trips can usually be found. Koreans themselves often use this method when away from home and their own cars. Taxis offer the option of much greater flexibility both in route and schedule, and can stop whenever and wherever the passengers want them to. Finally, some taxi drivers are willing to help with things like meals and ticket purchases.

Hire cars and self-drive rental cars are another option, of course. Cautions about driving in Korea mentioned in the previous chapter should be especially heeded if a long trip is planned. Those who do not speak Korean should have place names written down in Hangul or Chinese characters to avoid getting lost, although even then understanding directions given in Korean will be a problem. The adventuresome will find this a very interesting way to get around in the country, but they must be prepared to get lost and frustrated at times if they cannot speak and understand the language.

Where to stay in Seoul poses only the problem of a plethora of choices. The capital city has more than ten deluxe hotels (rooms US$50–125 per night, double or twin) as classified by the Korean National Tourism Corporation. The Lotte, the Westin Chosun and the Seoul Plaza are all in the heart of downtown; the Shilla, the Seoul Hilton and the Hyatt Regency are only slightly less conveniently located and all offer excellent views of the city; and the Sheraton Walker Hill, while further out, is in a lovely setting and has the fanciest nightclub and only gambling casino in the city.

Where to stay

All of the above offer the full range of services expected of an international class hotel, and all have good western, Korean, Chinese and Japanese food. As noted in the following chapter, good western food is expensive in Korea, and imported wines and liquor are very expensive. But for those willing to pay, superior accommodation is almost always available in Seoul.

Slightly below these hotels are the numerous first-class establishments (US$40–55) including the Seoulin, the Seoul Royal, the Mammoth and many others which offer more than adequate facilities. Several of these boast special features like live theater, popular nightclubs or convenient locations for shopping and tourism. All are clean, reasonably efficient and staffed by speakers of several foreign languages, especially English and Japanese.

Finally, Seoul has innumerable second-class (US$30–45) and third-class (US$25–40) hotels. With these foreign visitors take their chances. Some are perfectly adequate, some sub-standard; all are, in theory, regularly inspected for fire safety, but com-

pliance with regulations varies greatly. The food
provided in the less expensive places is generally less
attractive to westerners, although it can be fine. If one
happens to stumble upon a place much frequented by
prostitutes and their customers, late night and very
early morning hours can get rather interesting. Some
of these less exalted hotels can add a new dimension
to a Korean visit; some can impose unnecessary
burdens.

Going native   Seoul also has a great many Korean-style inns called
yogwan. The major features of such places are the
ondol floors (heated by air moving through channels
under the floors), traditional bedding consisting of a
thick pad used as a mattress (called a *yo*), a covering
quilt (called an *ibol*), and a very hard pillow made by
stuffing grain husks into a cover. Typically the rooms
are bare of furniture, although television sets can
sometimes be rented, and open on to a long, outdoor
porch. Toilet and washing facilities are communal,
but some *yogwan* provide private baths similar to the
Japanese *furo*.

Yogwan are a touch of the authentic old Korea, and
in fact most of them are not equipped to deal very
efficiently with foreigners. While interesting to try
once, *yogwan* are hard for many visitors to adjust to.
Sleeping on a heated floor during the winter is
uncomfortable for many, and using the traditional
hard Korean pillow can result quite literally in a pain
in the neck. Lounging around in such rooms is
difficult since there are no chairs or couches of any
sort; reading lights have not yet been introduced into
most *yogwan*.

At least three such places in Seoul are prepared to
cope with foreign guests who do not speak Korean:
the Undang, the Daiwon and the Daeji. All are
reasonably priced at US$7–9 per person per night.
One big problem is finding them, since most taxi
drivers will not recognize their names and will have
little idea how to find them. The easiest thing to do is
have a Korean speaker phone before the guests arrive
and then accompany them in the taxi to make sure
they arrive at the right place.

An even better idea is to skip the *yogwan* experience in Seoul, and try one at one of the tourist spots outside the city. For instance, a trip to Haein-sa from Seoul requires most of one day. Quarters can easily be found in Taegu (it has several perfectly adequate first-class hotels), but a more interesting night can be spent in the village next to the temple. The village is made up almost exclusively of *yogwan*, souvenir shops and small restaurants. Finding a place to sleep for the night is easy, even without knowing Korean. Much of the following day can be spent viewing the temple and its environs before the return to Seoul.

Yogwan are located in the immediate vicinity of nearly all tourist spots in South Korea. Kyongju and Sorak-san, for example, both have a great many within an 8 or 9 km radius of central sites. Both of these areas also have deluxe hotels (in Sorak village, the Park, and in Kyongju, the Kolon, the Chosun and the Tokyu) and less fancy, cheaper facilities as well. But both places also provide good opportunities for experiencing a *yogwan*.

Coping with luggage

Tourists with a great deal of luggage should avoid bus travel; most often highway express buses have room for only fairly small bags. Train travel with several bags is a bit easier since *Saemaul* and express trains usually have plenty of room in overhead racks. Overnight trips to see special sights will not require much baggage; excess bags can usually be stored in Seoul's better hotels until guests return. Longer trips will require more things, but formal dress is never required, and only a minimum of items need to be taken.

If a lot of luggage must be carried, travelers in Korea should be wary in train stations, both arriving and departing. Semi-official porters (they are paid no salary, but they are allowed on to platforms without tickets) inhabit all train stations, being especially numerous in Seoul. They are often quite aggressive about carrying bags, finding the right seats and procuring taxis, and as such they can be very helpful. They are, however, also quite aggressive about demanding fees for their work, sometimes very high fees. The rush and bustle of busy train stations can create an atmosphere in which exorbitant fees will be paid just to get out. Travelers should either be prepared to pay such fees or clearly establish rates before the work is done. Standing in a long queue for a taxi is sometimes better than being gouged.

Summary Visitors to Korea have many options open to them in terms of what to see, where to stay and how to get there. As in all countries, the more one pays, the more comfortable the accommodation, usually. Also, as a general rule, the more one pays, the more refined the company. If visitors want to see the things in Korea, then paying for comfort is a good decision. If the people of Korea are the major attraction, then a closer look can be found at lower prices.

Lower prices also mean, of course, putting up with crowds, public toilet and washing facilities, less clean quarters, using cold water and inferior food. Some people don't care about these things, others do. Fortunately for everyone, Korea offers the entire range from top to bottom. Cheap flophouses and greasy spoon restaurants coexist with international hotels and superior food service. One usually gets what one pays for in Korea.

Eating: the good things

Korea is famous for at least one dish, *kimchi*, and well known for several others, including *bulgogi*, *kalbi* and *bibimpap*. At its best, Korean food is among the finest in the world. Textures and tastes blend in surprising and complex ways to keep the diner interested and charmed.

Many characteristics of Korean food are shared with other Asian cuisines. The major tastes (garlic and spicy hotness), the primary methods of preparation and serving (most foods cut into bite-sized pieces and a large number of dishes served at every meal), the staples (rice and/or noodles and soups), the kinds of foods (predominance of vegetables and seafood and relatively little red meat), and the use of chopsticks, are all common to many varieties of Chinese, Japanese and Southeast Asian cuisines.

Chief specialities

However, as is true of all these other countries, Korea has distinctive, even unique aspects to its food. Above all else there is *kimchi*, best known in its very hot, very garlicky form made of cabbage, but in fact a complicated, multifarious dish that can be very mild – as is *mul* or water *kimchi* – and made from cucumbers, radishes, carrots, greens other than cabbage, or practically any other vegetable. The most remarkable thing about *kimchi* is that a great many Koreans, probably the vast majority, must have some of it with every meal, even if it is only a single small piece. It is ever present, mainly homemade, but also available canned for the hundreds of thousands of Koreans who live and work in other countries.

A visitor to Korea can make no more friendly gesture at a meal than to eat and enjoy *kimchi*. It is not necessary to eat a lot, and it is acceptable to mix it with rice and even to dip it into soup if it is too hot.

But eating an occasional small piece during a meal will make Korean hosts comfortable, and most foreigners can develop a taste for at least the milder forms in a short period of time.

Every fall, just as the weather begins to turn cold, the major ritual of *kimchi*-making takes place. Thousands of tons of cabbage, white radish, red pepper and garlic are needed at this time to provide the raw ingredients for the production of winter *kimchi*. The increased activity in vegetable markets is obvious, and the roads to major cities are clogged with farmers moving their goods to urban markets. This period, called *kimjang*, is an intriguing one for foreigners to observe, for although the practice of *kimchi* making is not quite so widespread as it once was, it is still impressive to see how many people are mobilized to the task.

Enjoying the other famous dishes of Korean cuisine, *bulgogi* and *kalbi*, will take little or no effort on the part of most visitors. *Bulgogi* is thinly sliced, marinated beef that in its classic form is cooked on a cone of iron which is heated from the inside. As the beef cooks, liquid collects in a trough at the base of the cone; additional liquid (water or stock) and vegetables can be added to the trough liquid to make a delicious soup. At its best, *bulgogi* is a marvelous dish worthy of its high reputation.

Kalbi is marinated beef short ribs that are baked at a low temperature for a long time until extremely tender. The spicing of *kalbi* varies from region to region, but ginger, soy and garlic are included in all versions. Either *kalbi* or *bulgogi* may serve as the centerpiece of a meal consisting of rice, *kimchi* and a large variety of other side dishes. With good beef properly marinated, either can produce an exquisite meal. Unfortunately, tender, aged beef is not often available in Korea outside the best and most expensive restaurants of Seoul and other large cities.

Bibimpap is a single bowl rice dish with various condiments on the side and an egg, often raw, on the top. The condiments – including hot pepper sauce, different greens, some *kimchi*, etc. – and the egg are stirred into the rice, which is hot, and the egg cooks slightly. The result is a very efficient, filling and tasty dish that is usually eaten with a spoon by Koreans, but can also be eaten with chopsticks by the diligent. This Korean version of fast food can provide relief for those weary of hot, spicy dishes because diners mix their own dishes to suit their own tastes.

Stalls on the streets sell other fast foods, especially a wide variety of soups, noodle dishes and steamed buns with meat and vegetable fillings. One particularly interesting dish is *naengmyon*, a cold noodle dish that is very spicy. The buckwheat noodles from which it is made are very long, and they must be cut to be served in manageable lengths. Sanitary conditions at most such stalls must be considered suspect at best, but for the more adventuresome, eating at the stalls with the masses of lunch time and evening diners is an unusual experience.

Other staples
Tubu

Bean curd – called *tubu* in Korea, *tofu* in Japan, and *doufu* in China – is a major element of the Korean diet. It is, frankly speaking, one of the most versatile and marvelous foods ever invented. It is very high in protein, very low in fat, and only moderately calorific. But far and away its most outstanding feature is its almost infinite flexibility; it lends itself to soups, salads, main dishes, snacks and desserts. It can be served hot or cold, sweet or sour, spicy or bland, dried or in liquid, alone, with sauce, or as a small part of a much larger dish of mixed meats, seafood, and vegetables.

Generally *tubu* in Korea comes in large blocks about 5 cm thick and 60 cm square; these blocks are cut up to give the customer the size of piece desired. These smaller pieces may be further processed at home by squeezing out most of the liquid, cutting into small strips, drying or by many other techniques. The results of additional processing may be boiled, fried, baked or eaten raw; it may be breaded, shredded or reduced to mush in a soup base. There does not seem to be any limit to what can be done with *tubu*, although the Koreans have not yet arrived at the point of making artificial ice cream from it like the Americans do.

Tubu in Korea is still a food that must, according to customary practice, be purchased and eaten fresh. Although some packaged, pasteurized forms have appeared in Korean supermarkets, it is mostly still bought daily and consumed on the day of purchase. *Tubu* is an immensely popular food in Korea, especially in soups. It is nearly as popular as *kimchi*, appearing in some form at almost every meal.

The popularity and requirement for freshness of *tubu* has given rise in Korea to an extensive production and distribution network that is dominated by small and moderate scale undertakings. The distribution system is particularly interesting, although its finer points can only be appreciated by someone who lives in a residential area with single-unit dwellings. In this context, *tubu* is an excellent example of a product that resists mechanization even in a rapidly industrializing society.

In residential areas, *tubu* is normally sold out of hand carts twice a day: very early in the morning, as early as 5.30 am during the summer, and in the evening, generally around 6.00 or 6.30 pm. The morning sales usually go into the morning meal and the evening sales into the evening meal. Koreans can be quite obsessive about the freshness of their *tubu*. The vendors of it are usually older women who have specified routes in residential areas. They walk through the streets ringing very distinctive sounding brass bells that identify who they are from a great distance away. By the time the vendor arrives at a corner, customers are waiting with dishes in hand to buy and take home the freshly made *tubu*.

Now one might imagine that some people would get rather irritated by having someone stand outside their house morning after morning ringing a very loud brass bell to hustle business. But it doesn't seem to bother most Koreans much; they have, in any case, grown up with the sound in their environment and are used to it. To newcomers from outside Korea, it can be extremely disruptive to be wakened every morning by the incessant clanging. A quaint custom perhaps, and even a charming reminder of simpler days, but nonetheless hard on sleep.

Korean fruit is a delight, especially the apples, which *Fresh fruit*
are grown in an amazing number of varieties, a
particular pear, huge, brownish gold in color with a
slightly rough skin, and a Korean variety of Mandarin
orange. Fresh fruit is very popular throughout the
country, being served as the final course to nearly all
dinners, but also eaten throughout the day as a snack.

Korean pears, which are similar to ones grown in
Japan, are a new experience for most outsiders. They
can be very large; up to 1 kg each is not unusual.
Their golden brown color is also quite different from
the yellows, greens and even reds familiar to westerners. But the most striking things about Korean pears
are their texture and juiciness. At their best, they are
exceptionally crisp, almost like a very good apple, but
the flavor is distinctly pear-like. The flesh of these
pears is very juicy – they can, in fact, be quite messy
to eat – and creamy white to translucent white in
color; truly a wonderful fruit.

Nearly all the fruit sold in Korea is grown
domestically, including occasional pineapples from
the southernmost island of Cheju. Only bananas are
imported in large numbers, and then with an astrono-
mical tariff. It is not unusual for a single banana to
cost US$3 on the streets of Korea. Strawberries are
also available for increasingly long periods and at ever
more reasonable prices, and a small, less tasty variety,
called *san* or mountain strawberry, is available at a
lower price and for a longer time.

In recent years, the widespread use of vinyl plastic
sheeting as ground cover and for hothouses has
dramatically improved the availability of vegetables
and some fruits, especially strawberries, but has had
little impact on production of most other fruits.
However, since Korea is a relatively small country
with a very good transportation system, fruits like
apples and pears need not be picked early, ripened
artificially and shipped great distances. For the most
part, tree fruits in Korea retain a fresh, natural flavor
even when served in the major cities.

Koreans never eat the skin of fruits. Apples and
pears are always peeled before eating, much as
bananas and oranges are. In fact, artistic peeling of

apples and pears is one of the finer culinary arts of the country. This is an example of making a virtue of a necessity, since Koreans see the skins of fruits as dirty and not fit to be eaten. At one time, this prejudice derived from the use of human excrement as fertilizer, still a practice in some areas, and now it is linked with the use of chemical fertilizers and pesticides. Foreigners used to eating the skins of fruits like apples and pears are likely to encounter rather startled responses if they do so in the presence of Koreans.

Properly speaking, Korean meals have only two courses: all the other food and drink, and the fruit. The fruit course announces the end of a meal; it is always the last course, and when the fruit is eaten the meal is over. This is a very handy custom in a society where the evening meal can take a very long time, but has little structure. The highly structured and formalized practice of ending with fruit is an aid to novices, helping them over one of the awkward hurdles of Korean dining.

Garlic   Korea is well known for the amount of garlic its people consume. Even visitors familiar with the amount of garlic included in other cuisines – Italian, Chinese and French, for example – leave Korea astounded by the amount and forms of garlic eaten in that country. It is also true that newcomers to Korea can smell garlic in the air as a general quality, independent of proximity to restaurants or other cooking and storage facilities. Awareness of this odor fades quickly, however.

A fine Korean meal, either in the home of the well-to-do or in an excellent Korean restaurant, may well serve garlic in ten different forms. Garlic soup made with whole bulbs is popular; raw garlic is served as an accompaniment to many different dishes; and grilled, sliced garlic bulbs are a new experience for most outsiders. In addition to these forms, many of the best Korean dishes are heavily flavored with garlic.

Garlic comes in many varieties and colors in Korea. One of the most potent kinds has a brilliant purple skin that leaves a faint tint in the cloves themselves.

Garlic is commonly sold in enormous long bunches bound together by coarse rope or its own stalks. Garlic stalls in local markets sell everything from the plants to bulbs, to whole cloves, to chopped cloves, to finely ground powder. These stalls are, obviously, pungent and interesting places.

Probably more even than the heavily spiced hot dishes like *kimchi*, visitors to Korea remember the garlic, and, of course, in a great many dishes, hot red pepper and garlic are both present. Koreans are somewhat sensitive to their reputation as garlic eaters – a derogatory term sometimes used by the Japanese to demean Koreans – and when serving guests, they will often reduce the amount of garlic put into foods. Many of their guests appreciate the courtesy.

When Koreans entertain guests, either at home or in restaurants, meals become rituals in which relationships are cemented and contacts secured. A formal Korean meal can easily consume hours, with a seemingly endless variety of dishes. Conversation is an important aspect of eating which contributes to the length of meals. In general, Korean dishes are not intended to be eaten either very hot or very cold, but rather at a lukewarm or slightly chilled temperature, so it is not necessary to rush their consumption. Leisurely is the word that best describes the style of dining at these meals.

Style of dining

One difficulty many westerners have at Korean meals is sitting at the low tables which are surrounded by cushions. Nearly all Korean homes and many of the best restaurants which serve Korean food use these low tables. In many cases diners are seated on cushions around an open space, and then tables are brought in and placed before them. After a lifetime of practice, Koreans can sit on the floor with legs crossed or with their legs bent under them or to the side for hours without noticeable discomfort.

Westerners, on the other hand, usually experience a great deal of discomfort from the very beginning, and some never adjust to the required posture. The only relief from this discomfort is to stretch one's legs out, but this frequently causes embarrassment in the form of upset tables. Koreans who have dined often with westerners recognize the difficulty and encourage their foreign guests to make themselves comfortable, and novices would be well advised to do just that. Quite intense pain can result if inexperienced knees are kept bent under stress for a couple of hours and then called upon to straighten out and walk.

A second difficulty may also arise. In order to make the seating arrangement intimate enough to allow the conversation that is a required part of a proper Korean meal, the tables around which guests sit are rather narrow. However, a large number of pots, plates and bowls are required to serve the wide variety of dishes that make up a typical Korean meal. It is normal for a single table with eight people around it to have as many as 20 or 30 serving dishes on it, often stacked on top of one another, plus individual rice and soup bowls and perhaps two or three kinds of drink. This makes for a precarious situation, especially when the foreign guests occasionally have to stretch their legs out in front of them to relieve pain and cramp. Upset dishes, spilled soup and even overturned tables do sometimes occur under these circumstances.

Obviously care must be exercised until one gets used to eating at low tables, and not just to avoid turning the table over. As in many other Asian countries, so too in Korea dishes set on the table are communal. That is, diners use their chopsticks to take small portions from dishes to their rice bowls or directly to their mouths. This means that people are constantly reaching and stretching, frequently nudging one another in the process. Once again, Koreans do all this quite adroitly, and gracefully even, while westerners can look a bit clumsy and feel even worse. Only practice and patience will remedy these problems, and fortunately they are rather easily resolved.

Chopsticks   The obstacle posed by chopsticks is usually not so easily overcome. Eating with chopsticks is a skill learned at a very young age in Asia, and it is one which requires a good deal of dexterity. Learning to use them as an adult is frustrating, embarrassing and time consuming. Besides, before the skill has been mastered, one can get quite hungry trying to rely on chopsticks for eating all meals.

A great many guides and instruction booklets are available to introduce the novice to chopsticks. The basic principle is simple: hold one stick reasonably steady, and move the other against the stable one. However, most food is very slippery, one's grip usually weakens after the food is off the plate or out of the bowl but before it has entered the mouth, and Koreans always seem to eat so effortlessly.

Perhaps unknowingly, Koreans can exacerbate the problems beginners with chopsticks have by giving them very narrow, very smooth metal ones which make picking up the small bits of food even harder. These metal chopsticks are lovely, and they do make the table setting more elegant, but they are very hard to use. For the beginner, the rough wooden chopsticks available in most cheaper restaurants or from street vendors are easier to use, as are the thick plastic kind that often have one slightly flattened side.

For the rank amateur, however, all styles of chopsticks are sources of clumsiness and frequent embarrassment. Remember always that if desperate hunger sets in, or if exhaustion and embarrassment get the better of one, Korean hosts will be happy to provide forks and spoons. But despite first impressions to the contrary, Korean food is most efficiently eaten with chopsticks. Besides, mastering this new skill is a source of minor pride for most visitors, and skill – even basic competence – in the use of chopsticks makes a favorable impression upon Korean hosts and friends.

Soup spoons

Soup is served with almost all Korean meals, and the utensil used to eat soup is a spoon with a long, narrow handle and slightly curved bowl. It is usually made of the same material the nearly impossible chopsticks are. Koreans typically eat a bit of rice, then a few bites with chopsticks, and then a little soup, all while holding chopsticks and spoon in the same hand, a procedure which requires considerable adroitness. Rice is sometimes eaten with the soup spoon also.

Toothpicks   Toothpicks commonly appear on dining tables in Korea, and many diners use them with gusto. However, it is considered very impolite to use a toothpick without covering the mouth with one hand while picking away with the other. The procedure is simple enough: when using a toothpick with one hand, simply raise the other hand in front of the mouth at a distance sufficient to allow room to work, but close enough to hide the open cavity. As a matter of curiosity, note that Koreans almost always have the toothpick in their right hands and cover their mouths with their left hands. This is because virtually all Koreans are right-handed; left-handedness is rarer there than in any western country.

A warning   A special caution is in order against one type of behavior: blowing one's nose at the dining table. While unusual and not polite in western society, this is seen as extremely impolite in Korea and may well cause revulsion in Korean diners. It is especially important to be aware of this problem because hot, spicy Korean food can often induce a runny nose in novices. Sniffing is acceptable, but taking out a tissue or a handkerchief and vigorously blowing one's nose is not; if the need becomes too pressing, excusing oneself from the table is the only solution.

Picnics   Since a great many Korean foods are not intended to be eaten either hot or cold, but rather lukewarm or cool, they lend themselves quite nicely to picnicking, which is very popular in Korea. One special dish, *gujul pan* – Nine Treasures – is especially well suited to picnics. Small strips of cooked egg yolk, egg white, beef, carrot, bean sprouts and other vegetables to a total of eight are served with thin crêpes, which constitute the ninth treasure. Picnickers take crêpes, fill them with their choice of goodies, deftly roll them up with chopsticks and eat them. This is a very colorful and tasty dish.

Actually, Korean picnics are often elaborate affairs, involving the carting of cooking facilities – *bulgogi* is also a popular picnic dish – into the wilderness. A great variety of vegetable, rice, cold meat and fish dishes are brought along to accompany the main item, which means that a great many containers are also needed. Altogether, a Korean picnic is a charming affair that someone has to do a great deal of work for, and the lucky foreign guest gets to enjoy.

Seoul has a number of high-quality western restaurants; at least one in each of the major hotels, and others not located in hotels. In the former category are the outstanding continental facilities in the Shilla, the Hilton and the Plaza. These, and several in other hotels, are the match of the major restaurants in nearly any hotel in Asia. The food is excellent, the service gracious, and the prices shocking. In Korea, the generally breath-taking prices of such establishments are greatly exaggerated by the outlandishly high cost of imported wines, which is the result of very high import duties.

Non-Korean restaurants

Outside the major hotels, other good western restaurants have also made an appearance in recent years. One of these, L'Opera, an Italian restaurant in the Saejong Cultural Center, is well worth a visit. Although associated with the Plaza Hotel, L'Opera is not in the same building and operates to a certain extent on a different supply system. Its prices, however, are nearly the match of better restaurants in the big hotels.

Unfortunately for the western visitor to Korea, good western restaurants still mean very high prices. Moving to a more moderate price range results in a major decline in quality. For the short-term guest, this is not a major weakness, since Korean food holds sufficient range and delights to fill weeks (although most westerners prefer to stick with western breakfasts). But for those who travel to Korea often or stay for long periods, the lack of reasonably priced western restaurants is a problem. Beyond Seoul, this shortage is even more apparent, and apart from the few other major cities and tourist areas – Pusan, Taegu, Kyongju and Cheju Island – there is no good western food available.

Japanese and Chinese food, both with special Korean variations, are available in numerous restaurants in all major cities. The Chinese food, particularly, is strongly influenced by Korean cuisine, and will be something of a surprise to those familiar with the Chinese food available in western countries, Japan, Taiwan or Hong Kong. Because of a much stronger and more recent Japanese influence, the Japanese food available in Korea is more familiar to outsiders.

There are virtually no other ethnic specialty restaurants in Korea. The ethnic uniformity of Korea, which has only very small and widely dispersed minority populations, makes it difficult for restaurants devoted to particular ethnic cuisines to be supported. Since there are no large concentrations of Indian, Indonesian, Vietnamese, Thai or other Asian peoples, to say nothing of Mexicans, Germans or Yugoslavs, restaurants specializing in foods from these places do not exist. This is one way in which Seoul differs markedly from other large Asian cities like Tokyo, Hong Kong, and Singapore.

Tipping   Generally speaking tipping is not required in restaurants in South Korea. Nearly all eating establishments add a 10 per cent charge to the bill for service, so no additional payment is expected. However, Koreans commonly leave small change that is returned from paying the bill, especially coins; and, if particularly attentive service or special assistance of some kind has been given to customers, a small tip is appropriate.

Western fast foods   In another way, however, South Korea is gradually becoming more like other large Asian cities with the advent in recent years of American fast food chains. Although there are still relatively few outlets, and as yet no McDonald's at all, the hamburger purveyors have arrived in the form of Burger King and the pizza mongers in the form of Pizza Hut. Altogether the country has 16 fast food chains in operation, 13 of which are affiliated with foreign companies.

Fast foods are nothing new to Korea, or to most other Asian countries for that matter. For hundreds, perhaps thousands, of years, food carts have been a fixture on the Asian scene. Various kinds of noodle dishes, soups and steamed buns filled with meats and vegetables have long been peddled on city streets. Take-away food is nothing new to Koreans.

It seems likely, given the experience of other Asian countries in recent years, that western-style fast food places will become increasingly popular. But there are some problems which will have to be overcome. Traditionally, Koreans have not liked either cheese or tomato sauces, making pizza a rather problematic dish. Younger Koreans, of course, need only to become used to these foods to make pizza and hamburger ventures a success in Korea as they have been in Japan, Hong Kong, Taiwan and elsewhere.

Meanwhile the odd western traveler starved for a little junk food can drop into one of the few outlets for a quick meal. The standards of the Korean outlets measure up to those elsewhere in Asia, as do the prices. As in the West, such eating places are the realm of the young, so those visitors wishing to see the old Korea should not expect to find it in a Pizza Hut.

There are other food shops in Korea that look like fast food places, especially fried chicken shops with names that approximate Kentucky Fried Chicken. One should be rather wary of these places, not only because the food is usually not very good but also because the standards of cleanliness are not high. Sometimes even easily identified logos of famous fast food outlets appear in the streets of Korea without really announcing the presence of the famous outlet. Deceptive advertising is rampant in the country, so let the buyer beware.

Eating: the other things

Eating is, obviously, a matter of taste. While it is rarely literally true that one man's meat is another man's poison, it certainly is true that some societies eat things that other societies find morally objectionable or, more often, not good. Foreigners coming to Korea are likely to run into many things that surprise them, and nowhere more often than when eating.

Koreans have traditionally eaten some things – especially dog and snake – that most visitors consider unacceptable as food. Numerous other things in the regular Korean diet are viewed by many foreigners as curious, untasty, or just overdone: both garlic and hot pepper fall into this last category.

What follows is an account of some of the things that might be encountered in Korea. All individuals will have to decide for themselves whether or not they like a particular item, of course, but the foods discussed here are ones a great many westerners have, for various reasons, found unpleasant in the past. The truly adventurous traveler will skip this chapter and enter the fray with no preconceptions; those hoping to reduce discomfort to themselves and their hosts will be forearmed by the following.

A special note: most South Koreans who have wide experience with foreigners are well aware of the latter's common prejudices, and will avoid serving things that might be objectionable, especially dog and snake. Occasionally, however, foreigners will encounter Koreans who enjoy serving things that probably will not be well received, because they find the strong reactions of foreigners humorous. This will occur only after close familiarity has been established; it will never happen to short-term or casual visitors.

These two things are included in both chapters on eating because they can be very good in moderate doses and very hard to take in heavy concentrations. People who find *kimchi* new and interesting at dinner may be quite nonplussed by having it served for breakfast also. Garlic is a delightful spice that is used throughout much of the world, and most people like it in small quantities. But sitting down to a table containing a grill with some meat and vegetables on it along with a hundred or so cloves of garlic is a surprise to some, and having dish after dish served with garlic in one form or another can be tiresome.

Garlic and kimchi

Generally, the best advice is to eat only what one likes. There are times, though, when some special effort will be required in order to avoid embarrassment. In these cases, remember that thoroughly cooked garlic cloves and bulbs do not taste as strong as raw ones and that it is acceptable to take some rice with a piece of *kimchi* or dip it discreetly into soup to cut the flavor a bit.

Classic winter *kimchi*, which has spent weeks to months ripening in a pot buried in the ground, can be a formidable food. The cabbage or white radish that serves as the base of winter *kimchi* loses its crispness, of course, and takes on a brownish-reddish hue from the peppers, garlic and ginger root with which it has been mixed. Winter *kimchi* also has a characteristic sharp odor of garlic, red pepper and pickled vegetable.

Even most Koreans eat only a little winter *kimchi* at one sitting, the amount varying greatly from individual to individual. *Kimchi* is definitely an acquired taste, and few foreigners ever catch up with the Koreans' love of the dish. Its strong flavor, pervasive odor and ubiquity can occasionally be oppressive.

In an effort to eliminate potential awkwardness during the Olympics in 1988, the Korean government began in 1984 to drive the dog and snake meat shops and restaurants from the main streets of Seoul. The project has been very successful, so much so that most visitors for these events will be unlikely to run

Dog and snake

across any such facilities. Those establishments which remain in Seoul are on remote back streets and hidden alleys. Finding one in the late 1980s requires considerable effort and a knowledgeable guide.

Why were the dog and snake shops driven out? Because the powers that be want foreign guests to remember Korea as new and modern, rather than quaint and unusual. If the eating of dog and snake is criticized or laughed at by western commentators, then it must be stopped, or at least removed from view. This attitude reflects considerable insecurity about what is good in Korea and what is bad. This potential source of embarrassment is fairly easy to control; others, like political demonstrations and their oppression, are harder to deal with.

The eating of dog and snake in Korea – and most of the rest of Asia, for that matter – is rooted in the belief that they provide health benefits. They are seen as nearly medicinal, and certainly beneficial in rather specific senses. What may be the major source of embarrassment to the Korean government is that, at least in the case of dog, the supposed benefits are primarily sexual. This traditionally reserved society is quite susceptible to embarrassment about public aspects of sexual matters.

Dog meat is typically eaten in Korea by men during the summer, especially during the hottest days of July and August, the so-called 'dog days' (the name does not come from the custom; rather it derives from the fact that during late July and August, the star Sirius, the brightest element of the constellation called *canis major*, rises and sets with the sun). Dog meat is supposed to increase virility, among other things, and it is especially favored by middle-aged men. It is interesting to note that in some parts of China, dog is favored mostly as a winter meal for women to provide resistance to cold.

Perhaps the government is concerned about increased virility in an already overpopulated country, but more likely it is simply responding to real or imagined mockery from foreigners. There is little internal pressure from groups concerned with the humane treatment of animals, and Korean men, in private, bemoan the loss of dog meat restaurants. This makes the theory of response to outside criticism all the more likely.

Snake is also seen as virtually medicinal by many Koreans. The ailments it is supposed to cure or ease are more wide-ranging than the ones that dog meat helps: general weakness, kidney and liver disorders, dissipation and a host of others. In fact, the view of the benefits of dog and snake meat fits in very well with the larger notion of traditional medicine in Korea.

Drawing heavily from the Chinese concept of medicine, Koreans have a wide variety of roots, herbs and foods that are consumed for medicinal purposes. Both the traditional Korean and the Chinese notions of medicine are closer to the western use of vitamins, food supplements and health foods than to the western view of symptom- and time-specific medicines. For Koreans, taking medicines consists of the long-term use of low dosages to prevent rather than cure disorders. To some extent, dog and snake meat fit into this scheme.

Be that as it may, in Seoul at least, the vendors of these things have been driven from view. Foreign visitors desiring experience with them will have to make a major effort or be disappointed. Actually, the elimination of dog and snake shops is no major loss to Korea except to the extent that it represents another step in the loss of uniqueness. It marks one more way in which Seoul is just a huge, modern city, rather than a huge, modern, Korean city.

Beef

As mentioned earlier, Korean beef is not a very high-quality product. Primarily because the country can ill afford the luxury of vast tracks of grazing land for beef cattle, it produces little beef. While some nutritionists would argue that this is to Korea's advantage, the demands of ever more foreign tourists, and the rapidly increasing demands of Koreans themselves, are gradually giving rise to a domestic beef cattle industry.

Meanwhile, nearly all good beef is imported (mostly from New Zealand and Australia), and therefore expensive. It can be had in the better restaurants in major cities, but is hard to come by elsewhere. The fact that Korea's two most famous beef dishes, *kalbi* and *bulgogi*, are both heavily marinated is a reflection of the general quality of domestic beef.

Kalbi and *bulgogi* should not be avoided; both are excellent dishes. But broiled beef steaks that are not imported are very likely to be tough and lacking in flavor. To compensate for this, restaurants using domestic beef very often overuse tenderizers, which also yields tasteless, poor textured steaks. Even hamburgers made from domestic beef have a flavor that most westerners find odd.

The tremendous influx of foreigners expected to accompany the Olympics will strain Korea's ability to provide sufficient beef (and dairy products also, though great advances have been made in this area in the past few years). Tourists are certain to be disappointed many times if they expect first-quality beef, so they would be well advised to eat other things. Korean cuisine has much to offer besides beef, especially seafood and vegetables, so skipping an occasional steak will impose no great hardship.

Dried cuttlefish

One of the favorite Korean snack foods is dried cuttlefish, a sea mollusk which resembles squid. Thousands of these things are sold every day in bulk by street vendors and in individual plastic packages on trains, in stations, etc. They can be seen in market areas piled high on carts, with a characteristic milky brown color and a distinctly 'fishy' odor.

While quite common as an accompaniment to drink, they are also consumed on their own by all kinds of people from children upwards. The dried, flattened carcass is torn into strips and eaten straight. They are especially popular as snack food during train and bus rides, particularly with women and their children.

This, too, is a taste which must be acquired. The dried cuttlefish are very salty, a result of the drying process, and they have a clear taste of fish. When thoroughly dried they have little odor, but the less

completely dried kind are favored by most people.
When not totally desiccated, the cuttlefish remain
supple and chewy, much like leather. The chewiness
and saltiness form the basis for their popularity, and
save for the saltiness, they have very good food value,
being high in protein, low in fat and calories.

Most westerners do not seem to like dried cuttlefish much, although some do. Visitors who make long
train or bus trips are almost certain to be offered some
by Koreans riding with them. If the cuttlefish simply
cannot be tolerated, polite refusal is possible, but
awkward. If it is accepted, tearing off a small piece to
taste is the wisest course. The texture makes them last
a long time, and if the chewer finds the taste
unpleasant, even a small piece feels like it swells to
enormous proportions.

Eat it all if it tastes good, surreptitiously slip the
remainder into a pocket or bag if it doesn't. Having
been offered a snack by fellow travelers, foreigners
will usually not be closely observed to make sure they
eat all of the gift. Be polite, return thanks, then cope
with the cuttlefish as required by personal taste. But
don't forget to clean out co at pockets promptly after
a trip; cuttlefish can leave a very strong smell.

One of the great delicacies of the coastal regions of
Korea is what is called live octopus and live fish.
Though these things are usually not really alive when
consumed, they may well have been sliced up while
alive only seconds before being served. In some cases,
the fish may actually remain alive for several minutes,
depending on how it is served.

Live octopus and live fish

As delicacies, these dishes are frequently served on
important occasions, such as when entertaining foreign guests. Thus it is possible, even likely, that visitors who have business to conduct in Korea's coastal
regions, or who will be entertained often by Koreans,
will eventually be served live fish or live octopus.
Being prepared for them will make it easier to
respond in a temperate manner.

Two distinct problems confront most westerners
the first time they encounter these dishes. One is
simply the idea of eating raw fish of any sort, served

any way. In many parts of the West, a recent major increase in the popularity of sushi and sashimi has introduced many people to the idea of eating raw fish. Also in many parts of the western world, raw oysters and occasionally raw clams are eaten, so the notion isn't completely strange. But still most people have at least a bit of a struggle the first time they try raw fish.

To some extent, it helps to make one's peace with consuming live fish or octopus by thinking of them as extremely fresh raw fish. One needn't worry much about refrigeration and possible food poisoning while eating fish this fresh. It will not have had time to spoil; its freshness is a palpable thing that cannot be denied or faked.

However, even if the widespread, initial aversion to eating raw fish is overcome, the second obstacle – the fact that the food is still quivering with life – is another matter. Having experienced this since child-hood, most Koreans aren't the least bit fazed by a quivering meal, but many visitors are. In fact, most are more than fazed, they are appalled, sometimes quite literally sickened.

How to cope? Well, if one likes raw fish already, in this form it is very good. Various kinds of fish are used, all of them delicious. So the promise of a culinary treat might help. If one does not like raw fish, either in theory or in practice, having it in this form will not change things. The only option is to pass up the dish politely and with as little display of aversion as possible.

Both dishes are usually served with a thick, very hot pepper sauce. Take a piece of fish, dip it in the sauce to taste, and eat it in one mouthful. The live octopus is eaten the same way, but poses a few minor problems. Although tasty, raw octopus is sometimes a bit tough, requiring a great deal of chewing. Also, the sucker pads on the tentacles can sometimes stick to the roof of the diner's mouth. In this case, shield the mouth with one hand and use a finger from the other hand to pry the tentacle loose, or work it loose with the tongue.

This all sounds a bit gruesome, but it is perfectly normal for Koreans, and many visitors learn to enjoy it also. Both the fish and the octopus are good, and both are healthy foods, especially if only a little of the hot sauce, which can be quite salty, is used. Besides, it is an adventure in eating the recounting of which will delight and/or appall friends who have not tried it.

Rotten fish

At least in one region of the country, there is a dish that is even more potentially offensive to foreigners than dog or live fish. In the southeast coastal regions, in the South Cholla province, a dish sometimes seen on special occasions features rotten fish, literally. Fish is purchased fresh and allowed to turn bad in a day or two of non-refrigerated storage. It is then sliced, uncooked, and eaten with the previously mentioned hot pepper sauce and lettuce or a similar green vegetable. Quite frankly, the smell alone is disgusting to people not used to the dish.

How one gets used to such a thing is a mystery; this is one dish the author has never tried. It seems to be eaten only by adult men and is accompanied by copious quantities of liquor, usually beer or the popular Korean drink called *soju* (which is similar to the *sake* of Japan). This does not seem to be a common dish, but most people from this particular area of the country know about it.

Paradoxically, to be at a meal where rotten fish is served is a sign of highest acceptance by Korean friends. All Koreans have a sense of how odd this dish is and how offensive foreigners find it. Therefore having it served in the presence of foreigners means that the Korean hosts have high respect for them, otherwise the dish is reserved for family members only. No Korean host is ever likely to offer this dish to foreign guests even if it appears on the table. Even finding out what it is can be difficult.

Mysteries

Koreans eat a great many things that are totally unfamiliar to westerners, mostly grasses and various vegetables. Things like bellflower root, young fern frond and fungi in abundant variety will appear at nearly every meal. Generally, Korean hosts are not able to come up with western names for these items, and even when they can, guests are not much the wiser for them.

A wide variety of seafood not usually eaten in the West also is popular in Korea. The specific variety of various clams, mussels, oysters and other mollusks may not be familiar, and sea urchins, sea horses and anemone will almost all be completely new. One such sea creature that foreign guests are bound to be served is sea cucumber, considered by most Koreans to be the supreme delicacy of the sea.

Sea cucumber (sometimes called sea slug by its numerous detractors, and widely known as *trepang* in its dried form) is popular throughout Asia. In Japan and China, also, it is considered high cuisine. Unfortunately many, if not most, westerners find it very difficult to like. When it is chopped up and mixed with other things – meats, vegetables, fish – it is fairly easy to overlook since it does not have a particularly strong flavor. But as a highly valued, and expensive, delicacy, sea cucumber is often served whole with a viscous sauce.

The main problem with sea cucumber is texture. To the eye, a sea cucumber seems soft and rubbery; to the mouth, it seems soft and crunchy. This latter may sound like a contradiction, but it is a very common description given by people trying sea cucumber for the first time. Combined with this is the blandness of the creature, which makes its taste quite unremarkable. Most visitors, even those who learn to tolerate sea cucumber, remain mystified as to why it is so highly thought of by Asians.

Preparation and variety

Beyond the raw ingredients of Korean food are problems with methods of preparation and the question of variety. As for preparation, the main weakness of much Korean food is that it has a very high salt content. Winter *kimchi* is especially salty, and most soups also have a great deal of salt. Soy sauce, which is exceptionally high in sodium, is used abundantly in Korean cooking. Dried cuttlefish has a high salt content also.

People on low sodium diets should be careful about eating too much of the kind of Korean foods that have a high salt content. Since most of the popular dishes fall into this category, strict adherence to a low sodium diet is difficult, especially for someone who wants to sample the delights of Korean cuisine. Bland food can be had in the country, but only at the expense of missing out on one of the more intriguing aspects of the culture.

Another problem with Korean food is the fact that, traditionally, all meals are comprised of the same elements: namely, soup, rice, a variety of side dishes, and perhaps a central meat dish or two. One is almost as likely to get *bulgogi* for breakfast as for dinner in a Korean home. In fact, breakfast often consists of leftovers from the previous evening's dinner.

Most westerners are used to clearer distinctions of content in a day's three meals, especially breakfast. Thus, most visitors to Korea prefer sticking with a western-style breakfast – eggs, cereal, toast, bacon, ham, fruit, etc. – even if they are very fond of Korean food. Thus, too, Korean food fascinates for a few days, but a steady diet of it must be relieved by western food once in a while. A continuous diet of Korean meals easily gets monotonous.

Cautions

Handling and storage of food in Korea have improved enormously in recent years. In most parts of the country, especially those frequented by foreign tourists, there is little to fear from food poisoning or other illnesses. Milk is pasteurized and all other dairy products are made of pasteurized milk. Fruits and vegetables should be well cleaned, but peeling and cooking everything is not necessary.

However, some cautions are in order. Raw fish is notoriously difficult to keep fresh, and since refrigeration is still not universally in use, care should be exercised about when and where raw fish is eaten. In private homes, of course, there is nothing to worry about. In restaurants or fish stalls close to the sea, raw fish is usually safe. But in the summertime, and at some remove from the sea, the dangers of infection increase. Common sense should be the guide when it comes to raw fish anywhere.

A more particular problem is the matter of fresh

water fish. Some years ago, Korea had a major infestation of liver flukes in fresh water fish. These creatures pose a potential danger to humans if the fish bearing them is not properly prepared. To be entirely safe, domestic fresh water fish should not be eaten at all, but the danger is now quite minimal.

Koreans are, on the whole, very conscious of the dangers of food poisoning and other food related problems. Foreign visitors can safely take their lead from Korean hosts and friends. While on their own, tourists should exercise the same prudent judgement needed anywhere. Places that look clean are more likely to be clean; places that are very popular probably do not regularly make their customers ill.

Finally, the matter of water. Koreans never, or at least very rarely, drink water that has not been boiled. While this practice now may have more to do with custom than need, water-borne ailments still do afflict many incautious visitors to Korea. Again, follow the lead of Koreans, who drink mostly water that has been boiled and then flavored with barley. Or drink tea, coffee or bottled beverages, all of which are perfectly safe. Cautions about the consumption of other liquids are offered in the following chapter.

Drinking: a national sport

Korea probably has more drinking establishments (serving alcoholic and non-alcoholic beverages) per capita than any other country in Asia. In addition to numerous bars and liquor houses, there are hundreds of places called *tabang* or *tashil*, which serve primarily coffee and tea, but also some light snacks. The local *tabang* is a favorite setting for Korean television soap operas (of which there are many), and is virtually a national institution.

The country also has a very active and prosperous liquor industry. Its products include at least three beers, many brands of inferior and one quite nice grape wine, various kinds of whiskies and rums, and two traditional liquors: *soju* and *makkolli*. These items are sold by the bottle in stores and shops, and by the bottle and drink in places ranging from very cheap *makkolli* shops to very expensive, fancy hotel bars, and the even more expensive hostess bars and *kisaeng* houses.

Like most countries, Korea has its own particular set of laws, informal rules and customs surrounding drink. *Tabang* are largely the preserve of the young, but far from exclusively; women do not drink much alcohol, but this is changing somewhat; and hostess bars and *kisaeng* houses, obviously, have only male customers. Whenever alcohol is consumed, something must also be eaten, even if it is only the smallest snack. Public drunkenness is frowned upon, but drunks are tolerated. Business and liquor are inseparably linked. All in all, drink is a complicated and fascinating aspect of Korean life.

Tabang and tashil

Coffee houses are by no means unique to Korea, but in very few countries are they so important. It is safe to say that after the home and family, they are one of the most important social institutions in the nation. Certainly for Korea's large student population, *tabang* are the major meeting places. But they are also very popular sites for informal business meetings, gossip sessions, trysts for lovers, and quiet talk among old and new friends.

Tabang are very tolerant places. Something – a cup of coffee or tea, at least – must be ordered upon arrival, but that entitles a customer to sit as long as he or she likes. The average customer of a Korean coffee house probably stays at least an hour, but a great many stay much longer. In most *tabang*, one is never pressed to buy more than an initial cup, no matter how long one stays.

The atmosphere in *tabang* varies greatly. Some are brightly lit, plastic and noisy; others are dim, have large, comfortable chairs, and are very subdued. Some feature rock music and are dominated by young university students; others play traditional Korean or classical music and cater to middle-aged businessmen and female shoppers.

Since most are located in busy commercial rather than residential areas, *tabang* are not quite like pubs or neighborhood bars in the West. The customers in most are almost equally split between regulars and casual drop-ins. This means that outsiders are not only welcome, but also rarely get the feeling that they are intruding on the private preserve of local residents. Most *tabang* have a mixture of customers who know each other and the staff very well and those who are virtually anonymous.

This mixture makes *tabang* intriguing places in which to observe an important aspect of Korean social life. Foreigners are usually made to feel very welcome, and are often given the best seating. But they are also usually left alone once they have been seated, have ordered and been served. From there on, foreigners can peer and eavesdrop at their leisure.

Not knowing the language drastically limits how much can be deciphered of what goes on in a *tabang*. Nonetheless, close observations of the comings and goings, gesticulations and expressions of the highly fluid clientele will provide outsiders with a view of the way many Koreans spend large amounts of their non-work time. In an otherwise very private society which is home, family and work centered, *tabang* offer a rare opportunity to get to know about Koreans on a personal level.

One sort of intrusion upon foreigners does sometimes occur in *tabang*. Many Korean university students are eager, even aggressive about practicing foreign languages. Thus it is not uncommon for foreigners to be approached in a *tabang* and engaged in conversation. Sometimes the students very openly ask if they can practice their language skills with foreigners; sometimes they are less straightforward about it. Very often, one student breaks the ice and others join in later.

Language students

Usually it is English that is practiced in this way, since it is far and away the most commonly studied foreign language. However, especially in Seoul, students also seek out French and German speakers. Though both of these languages rank far behind English in nationwide popularity, they have fairly strong followings in the capital city. This is particularly true of those *tabang* in the areas around the Seoul offices of the Goethe Institute and the Alliance française.

Being called upon to provide free language lessons can be a bore, of course, if it happens too often. But it can also be a very good opportunity to establish personal contacts with Koreans on an informal level. Quite naturally, Korean students are less formal when speaking English, say, than when speaking their own language. They can also be surprisingly forthcoming in criticism of their own country and government and brutally frank in their evaluations of international affairs and other countries. Making these sorts of connection can make a visit to Korea a much richer experience.

Prices in most *tabang* are quite reasonable, with a cup of coffee costing about the equivalent of US50¢. The fancier coffee houses in large hotels will usually charge twice that. Many *tabang* serve freshly brewed

Prices and quality of refreshments

coffee, but some have only instant. Koreans tend to use a lot of sugar and powdered cream substitutes in their coffee. Many, in fact, have no idea that the powdered stuff they add to their coffee is a substitute for milk or cream, having never used anything else.

Alcoholic drinks Three different beers are brewed in Korea: Crown, OB (Oriental Brewery) and Heineken. All have the same alcoholic content (about 5–6 per cent), all are light, and all are unremarkable. They have the blandness of American beers, rather than the distinctive flavors of European or Japanese beers. They are different from one another, and most people have a preference, but those who care enough and can afford it, prefer imported beers.

Crown and OB both have company-owned beer houses which serve only the owner's brand. These vary in size from rather small to rather large, although none yet matches the huge beer houses of Germany. These establishments serve draft beer in several mug sizes, snacks and, in some cases, meals. In atmosphere, most are convivial and noisy most of the day and downright raucous at night. Customers are mostly male, but increasing numbers of women are going to them also.

Most restaurants in Korea sell either Crown or OB; few sell both. The two breweries engage in stiff competition for exclusive outlets. Because Heineken is still slightly more expensive, it is sometimes available in places that exclude one or the other of the Korean beers. Only the best restaurants in major hotels offer all three, and sometimes one or two imports are available as well, usually Japanese, but occasionally American, and in a few places, San Miguel is sold too.

While not among the world leaders in per capita consumption of beer, Korea has produced its own beers for some time, and they are widely available. Beer goes well with most Korean foods, especially the very hot and salty ones. Koreans generally prefer their beer cold, thus according more with the tastes of Americans and Australians than those of the British and Germans.

A variety of beverages with higher alcoholic content is also produced in Korea. Their major attraction is that they are much cheaper than imported whiskies, Scotch, brandy, vodka and other hard liquors. The Korean brands are rarely preferred even by Koreans on the grounds of superior taste. Koreans who can afford such luxuries are quite snobbish about drinking imported liquor. One of the best gifts to give Korean male business or professional contacts is a bottle of Johnny Walker Black Label Scotch.

Korea also manufactures a variety of fruit wines, brandies and liqueurs, some of which are quite good. Home-brewed plum brandy is very common, ranging in quality from barely tolerable to delicious. Most of these products are very fruity in taste and usually rather sweet. In small quantities, they are nice, blending well with Korean foods; consumed in large quantities, they can be devastating. Grape wines are also made in Korea. In general, the red wines are not very good; some are too sweet, some are immature, some just taste bad. One kind of white wine, Majuang, is respectable. Made from riesling grapes, it is smooth, consistent, semi-dry and pleasant. Its price makes it competitive with foreign imports, which are subject to very high duties (more than 300 per cent in some cases). It is also much more widely available than foreign wines.

The more authentically Korean alcoholic beverages are *soju* and *makkolli*. Both are derived from rice; both are produced commercially and at home; both can be quite high in alcohol, ranging from 20 per cent to as high as 60 per cent. They differ in degree of refinement and distillation, *soju* being a clear liquid, *makkolli* milky. Older and more traditional Koreans generally prefer them to the western-style drinks.

Soju is similar to Japanese *sake*, and is, like *sake*, often drunk warm. Also like *sake*, *soju* is deceptively mild tasting while packing a powerful alcoholic punch. The consumption of *soju* in Korea, however, does not involve the elaborate ritual of *sake* drinking in Japan. *Soju* is usually sold in fairly large, clear glass

Local rice derivatives

bottles that have a slight blue-green tint. It can be transferred to smaller ceramic pots for warming or simply drunk at room temperature. *Soju* is now usually produced commercially and meets government standards of purity and alcoholic content.

The same cannot be said of *makkolli*. At its worst, it is a vile, dangerous brew that leaves an unappetizing sediment in bottles, glasses and stomachs. It survives only because poverty does also, and because some people will drink anything. Even an official publication of the Korean government's tourism office can only argue that at its best, *makkolli* 'has a not too unpleasant taste'. Nonetheless, *makkolli* remains very popular in Korea.

Its popularity is based mostly on low price, but also derives from tradition and the cultural complex that surrounds the drink. *Makkolli* houses are very numerous, especially in lower-class sections of cities and towns. In function, if not in tone, they are like some pubs in England, serving as neighborhood focal points, at least for men. These places generally also serve food, especially *pindaeduk*, a pancake with vegetables mixed into the batter, and *maeuntang*, a very hot fish soup. Always noisy, *makkolli* houses can become disorderly as the evening wears on and the *makkolli* dulls inhibitions.

Except in the remote countryside, women are not included in the ritual of *makkolli* consumption, which is one of few ways in which Korean women are fortunate. Although Korea does not have a major problem with alcoholism or public drunkenness, *makkolli* consumption is still an unsavory feature of social life there. Several times a year, newspapers carry reports of mass illness and even poisoning resulting from contaminated *makkolli*. It is sold in cheap plastic bottles that cannot be sterilized but are reused, or it is dipped from a common vat that is not very sanitary either.

While *makkolli* houses are doubtless an authentic part of Korea's quaint and unique past, they are not admirable institutions to be protected and promoted. They are too popular to close down by fiat, and would only become a worse social ill if made illegal.

But they are nothing for Korea to be proud of; it can only be hoped that increasing national prosperity will cause them to disappear of their own accord.

All imported alcoholic beverages in Korea are subject to very high duties, especially, as mentioned above, wines. These duties can more than triple the price of imported liquor, making it prohibitively expensive for most Koreans and dear for most tourists. It is possible that some of these duties will be lowered, at least temporarily, for the period of the Olympics, but the duties are a significant source of income for the Korean government, and therefore are not likely to be done away with or kept permanently low.

Imported liquors

High prices are especially noticed on wine lists in major hotels. Wines that sell for US$10 or $12 in the United States or French wines in the same price range can easily sell for US$40 in Korea. Better foreign wines are often sold for the equivalent of US$80–120, and the best wines of California and France are not available at all. Westerners who are used to having wine with their meals regularly find that wine accounts for half or more of their dinner check.

Cognac and armagnac are even more expensive. A single glass of a nice cognac can easily cost the equivalent of US$30 or more. This means that a pleasant meal with a drink before, wine during, and cognac afterwards might well come to US$200 or more: a ghastly price, and certainly not one that any but the richest tourists can afford even once. Even considering that most such meals are on business expense accounts, Korea must be counted an extraordinarily expensive place to drink and dine even modestly well in the western fashion.

Of course, one need not drink imported alcoholic beverages. But if Korea wants to attract more foreign tourists, the government should give serious thought to dropping some of these onerous duties a bit. Tourists should be very wary in fancy restaurants, checking prices carefully, and taking time to convert from Korean won to the appropriate foreign currency equivalent. A bill filled with naively ordered drinks can be a real shock in Seoul.

Hostess bars and *kisaeng* houses

The absolute top of the drinking and dining expense list in Korea are hostess bars and the increasingly rare *kisaeng* houses. The latter are similar to Japan's geisha houses, and now are at least as rare. Few foreigners except high-ranking businessmen invited by their Korean contacts know of or can afford to go to *kisaeng* houses.

Hostess bars in Korea are very much like hostess bars everywhere else. Patrons pay outrageous prices for drinks and get the company of one or more bar girls included. Depending on the class of the bar and the cost of the drinks, the company of these women can be as innocent as flirtatious conversation or as serious as a night-long private session. Here it is paramount that the buyer beware. First of all, customers should ascertain prices before the fun begins. Second, foreigners should not be fooled by appearances and their own false assumptions. Not by any means are all of these bars fronts for prostitution. In most, customers buy only the company and conversation of hostesses, not use of their bodies.

Kisaeng houses are a dying institution in Korea, and they have been since before the turn of the century. They grew out of a highly stratified, male-dominated society with an extremely wealthy elite class, and, in the long run, they can only be supported by such a society. As Korea is modernized and becomes more democratic, achieving a more equitable distribution of income, with archaic and immoderate institutions being subjected to closer scrutiny, *kisaeng* houses slowly disappear. Even more important to their demise are the economic factors. Given the competition of factory and office jobs, very few girls are attracted to the life of the *kisaeng* house, and the cost of maintaining one has increased enormously.

Traditionally, the girls and women of the places were multi-talented (singing, dancing, playing musical instruments, carrying on conversation, etc.), and the training program was rigorous. As with the Japanese geishas, so, too, were Korean *kisaengs* expected to be elegant, highly skilled, beautiful and refined. Their entire lives were dedicated to this profession, and they often started their training at quite a young age.

Not only were the women required to meet high standards, the food, drink and surroundings had also to be of excellent quality. The expenses of the *kisaeng* house were very high, even when labor and materials were cheap. Once labor became more expensive as a result of industrialization and a general increase in national prosperity, *kisaeng* houses could not be maintained except at extraordinary cost.

While there had always been various qualities of houses, increasing costs brought across the board declines in quality and the eventual disappearance of most houses. Their number shrinks every year as prices go up and new girls are not available for training. Now there are probably fewer than 20 establishments in Korea which can be called *kisaeng* houses even by stretching the definition. Very few of these are exclusively *kisaeng*, most being restaurants that also provide this service. Traditions die hard, of course, but *kisaeng* houses are gradually fading away.

Those that survive are extremely expensive. A typical evening of drink, dinner, and entertainment costs a minimum of US$150 per person, and can be as high as several hundred dollars each. Guests are attended to by women who prepare food, serve it, keep drink glasses filled, make conversation, provide musical entertainment, and in some cases offer romantic attentions (rarely more than caresses, however). Most western men are, in fact, made quite uncomfortable by such a flood of attention, but some adapt quite well. The language barrier often seems only a minor problem.

Simple tourists are very unlikely to go to a *kisaeng* house, since arranging an evening at one usually requires personal contacts. Businessmen and longer-term foreign residents of Korea might be invited to a *kisaeng* party by a wealthy contact, but even this is increasingly unusual. It is, furthermore, the sort of entertainment that is difficult to reciprocate. Finally, women other than the *kisaeng*, especially spouses of the male guests, complicate such evenings enormously.

An evening at a *kisaeng* house is an indulgence of a bygone era. While it retains a certain romantic and mysterious appeal for some, and for many foreign males would be a unique experience, it is not a required experience for understanding and enjoying Korea. To find out what most Koreans do in the evening, watch television; to find out what most Korean men do outside the home in the evening, go to an inexpensive restaurant or a *makkolli* house. To find out how many Korean men wish they could spend a night out, drop a bundle at a *kisaeng* house.

The ritual of drinking

When Korean men gather for dinner and drink, a fascinating ritual takes place. Everyone starts with his own drink and chooses for himself, perhaps wine, plum wine, beer, *soju*, or whisky; usually several different drinks are available. It is even acceptable, although unusual, to choose non-alcoholic drinks. Things generally start out slowly with introductions, if necessary, and light conversation. At this stage, there is frequently no particular focal point, but rather several small conversational groups getting warmed up.

Shortly after the meal begins, perhaps even before a central dish like *bulgogi* has been served, things begin to start moving, gently at first, but with increasing speed for the next 20 minutes or so. What happens is that when someone finishes his own first drink, he holds his glass upside down (to demonstrate that it is empty), and then hands it to another diner, while at the same time offering to fill it with a bottle of whatever is close at hand (try to remember to use two hands for all this passing, pouring and toasting). Note that this leaves the first person without a glass, and leaves the recipient of his glass with two.

Those diners experienced at this almost immediately pass on their own glasses as soon as they receive one, either giving it to the same person who gave them one, or involving someone else. When it is working perfectly, that is, when everyone at the table is of roughly equal status and familiar with the procedure, glasses pass from person to person smoothly and often. Within 20 minutes to half an hour, everyone at a table for eight or ten has drunk from someone else's glass and passed his own to another man, at least once, and usually several times.

This technique frequently results in the consumption of a great deal of drink. But it also creates a very convivial atmosphere and includes the entire table in the festivities. Newcomers are easily included into older established groups, and the shy are made to feel part of the group. The dinner can then continue to its conclusion with everyone happy and all social obligations fulfilled.

Unfortunately for the novice, this practice is fraught with pitfalls. First of all, if your drink is whisky, beware. Being passed three or four glasses in 20–30 minutes, and having them filled with strong drink, and being expected to down them, will strain any but the most hardened drinker. *Soju* is not much better, but wine is easier and beer even better. *Soju* and the fruit brandies that are popular in Korea are actually scarcely less alcoholic than is whisky, and they are sneaky, coming upon the unsuspecting with a real shock.

Second, in order to survive at this game, learn to pass glasses along as soon as you get them. The dilatory recipient of glasses will soon find himself with five or six arrayed before his place at the table, expected to pass them along as soon as possible. Well, maybe expected to pass them along; foreigners are given a lot of leeway. Not only are they not expected to drink everything put into their glasses, but they are also allowed to drink a little, and then pour the remainder of the drink into an empty water glass, or some other available receptacle.

A special problem is posed by the fact that foreign guests are very often the special targets of passed glasses because they are frequently the guests of honor. Everyone else at the table gangs up on the guest of honor when it comes to passing glasses. This means that special caution is often required of foreign guests.

The fact is, this is largely a matter of ritual. It's the form, not the content that is truly important, and the newcomer who quickly becomes skilled at the form will be in good shape from the beginning. On the other hand, novices who try to drink all of every drink passed to them – and the glasses will always be filled to the very brim – is in danger of an early, and indelicate, departure from the meal. It is very easy to get trapped by the setting and a desire to be one of the boys. This is understandable, but dangerous.

Actually, teetotalers are perfectly safe. Not indulging in the orgy of consumption is acceptable; people who don't drink will simply be skipped when it comes to the glass passing ritual. This may well leave the guest of honor out of the main action of the party, but it will also cool things off somewhat.

Sanitary considerations don't seem to be very important in this ritual. Those who are squeamish about such things will find themselves in an awkward situation, since the social pressure to participate is very strong. Non-drinkers are easily and graciously excused, but declining on the grounds of sanitation might be considered insulting. Whether or not the new fears of AIDS contamination will alter this practice remains to be seen. For now, however, the ritual continues.

Shopping

Korea is a shoppers' paradise for specific items. Fabrics and clothing, running shoes, old and new furniture and ceramics, semi-precious stones and jewelry made from them, ginseng and brassware are the major ones. Seoul is the most convenient place for foreigners to shop, and it has the widest selection of goods. Shopping outside Seoul – especially for antiques – can be rewarding, but it is also generally harder to do because of transportation and language problems.

Among the things that are not good buys in Korea are electronics, cameras, precious stones and jewelry made from them. Domestic manufacturers of the first two items are protected by very high tariffs which make imports prohibitively expensive. At the same time, domestically produced electronics (television sets, stereos, etc.) are not quite up to the standards of Japanese, European and American products. Korea produces only semi-precious stones, mostly amethyst, smoky topaz and jadite, so all precious stones are imported, and thus better purchased elsewhere.

Shopping in Korea is a matter of knowing how, what and where to buy. Bargaining over price is the norm (except in department stores), quality of products can vary greatly, and some locales are better for some items than others. Knowing what one wants and how much it should cost will help the naive shopper in Korea.

Money

The value of the won fluctuates against international currencies, and is especially sensitive to the US dollar rate; in early 1987, the exchange rate was over W850 to US$1. The won is not, however, a free floating currency, being very closely monitored and controlled by the central government.

Won circulate in coins and banknotes. The former are still minted in values of 1, 5, 10, 50, 100 and 500, while the latter are printed in values of 500, 1,000, 5,000 and 10,000. At an exchange rate of W850 to US$1, W1 coins are obviously of little value, and even a W10 coin is hardly useful, except for making telephone calls. Coins of W100 are the most common, and can be used in vending machines and for small purchases. Coins vary in size and material, while bills vary in size and color; all are easy to distinguish.

Outside the main hotels and shopping areas, Korea is a cash country. Credit cards are confined to large cities; personal checks are scarcely used, and travelers' checks can be exchanged only at banks and major hotels (the latter at unfavorable rates). While there is no limit on the amount of foreign currency that can be exchanged, reconversion in excess of US$100 must be accompanied by exchange receipts, and won may not be taken from the country.

There is a currency black market in Korea, and in many places transactions can be conducted in US dollars or Japanese yen. US dollars, especially, circulate widely in the country, and Koreans of the middle income class and above never seem to have any trouble getting hold of large numbers of US$100 bills. However, dealings in currencies other than the won are illegal and should be avoided by tourists.

How to shop
Bargaining or haggling is the order of the day in Korean shopping. Except for cigarettes, gum and similar small item purchases, outside grocery and department stores nearly all transactions are conducted on this basis. Several tips will help those unfamiliar with bargaining to understand what is going on.

Buy low, sell high applies to the Korean goods market as well as to any stock market. Merchants, small and large, are earning a living by what they do, and it is obviously to their advantage to get the best price they can. Generally, marked prices or the first price mentioned have a lot of room for downward movement, but if the customer is willing to pay the first price, the merchant is willing to accept it. Bargaining is expected.

Merchants who bargain start out with at least three advantages over their customers, especially the tourists among them. First, merchants do this all day, every day, and their survival depends on it. They are, therefore, both highly experienced and highly motivated. Tourists may be after a good deal, but their livelihood doesn't depend on making one, and neither do they bargain all day, every day.

Second, merchants and their help usually have a pretty good idea of the cost and quality of the items they are selling. This gives them an advantage in the bargaining process because they know where the bottom is. Only customers who have done extensive comparison shopping, or who have special knowledge, can approach the haggling procedure with the same confidence as the merchant does.

Third, merchants often have more flexibility in price because they sell things all the time, sometimes for higher prices, sometimes for lower. By contrast, customers most often conduct only a very limited number of transactions for a specific kind of item, usually only one. Thus a merchant may be able to go low on price because the last sale went high, or because moving the particular item out of stock is more important than a high price. On the other hand, merchants may be able to hold firm at a high price because other customers are interested or the item is not readily available elsewhere. Customers normally do not have this flexibility.

Not all the advantages are with the merchants, however. The major advantage the customer has is that merchants must sell to survive. A small profit is better than none, so selling low is better than not selling at all. And selling breeds selling, especially in the environment of an open-air market place. Potential customers are attracted by seeing a sale being made; they can be suspicious of an empty shop or stall.

Several guidelines will help novice bargainers. First, know the product: price, quality, availability, extent of usefulness or desirability. This knowledge is usually obtained by comparison shopping, but may also come from understanding one's own desires and needs before the bargaining begins. A low price may encourage the purchase of unwanted or unnecessary items, but the shopper should be aware that this is happening when it does. A good price on a useless item is no bargain.

Time can also be a weapon in the shopper's arsenal. If Aunt Tillie must have a souvenir of Korea, and shopping for it is done on the last day of a visit, a good price is unlikely. Be prepared when bargaining to walk away from the shop, to take time to reconsider, to look elsewhere. Merchants are more willing to yield when they realize the customer is not working under the pressure of time constraints.

Easily making mental conversions from one currency to another is also to the shopper's advantage. Some people like to work in units of hundreds or thousands. For example, these people fix in their minds that W1,000 is equivalent to a little more than 70 p sterling; so if an item is offered at W60,000, they can quickly convert that to a bit over £42 (70 times 60 equals 4,200 pence, or £42). Other people like to work with other forms of conversion. For instance, in converting from won to US dollars at a 900 to one rate, it is easy to divide the won price by 1,000 and then to add 10 per cent. Thus, an item that costs W40,000 converts easily to US$44 (40,000 divided by 1,000 equals 40 plus 10 per cent equals 44; at 900 to one the actual conversion is US$44.44). Whatever method seems simplest should be used consistently. This is especially important for people visiting several different countries in a short period of time.

Finally, understanding what is going on when bargaining will help make customers more comfortable with the process. Merchants want to get high prices, of course, but they usually are not trying to cheat customers. Bargaining can best be understood as a process of mutual face-saving, with the merchant making a profit and the customer getting a good deal. The perfect transaction leaves both sides happy.

Of course, some people simply cannot or will not bargain. They decide what a good price for an item is, and if that is offered, they buy; if not, they don't. This method can work in Korea, but it leaves out an intriguing and exciting aspect of the country. Bargaining is not exactly a game, rather it is more like a professional sport. Taking part in the process can give tourists an insight into how the country functions.

What to buy

Korea produces an enormous amount of clothing for sale in the West: silk dresses and shirts, cotton pants and skirts, all manner of clothing made from synthetic fabrics. Overruns and seconds are available at very good prices in shops designated as outlets and in large, outdoor markets that survive on the surplus and rejects of others.

Prices on such items can be very good, sometimes as low as one-third of the overseas price. Standard western sizes are usually available, although larger sizes are hard to find. Most shop keepers and vendors are familiar with the different sizing systems of the United States, the United Kingdom and Europe. In outdoor markets, insuring proper fit can be a major problem, since changing rooms are usually not available. Low prices can, however, justify taking a chance.

Curiously, Korean department stores are not especially good places to shop for ready-made clothes produced in the country. Most such items are intended for the export market, and taxing and marketing laws reflect this intention. Shoppers should not assume that items made in Korea will cost less in Korean stores than they will overseas, especially not silk items. In open markets and seconds stalls they usually do, but not in department stores.

Fabrics, particularly silk and cotton, can be good buys in Korea. The country has its own raw silk industry and exports it to other countries, for instance, Thailand. It does not have its own cotton fields, but a favorable labor and investment environment has for years allowed South Korea to import raw cotton and convert it into cloth and finished goods at very reasonable rates. For much the same reasons, synthetic fabrics are often an even better deal.

Tailor-made clothing is not a major item in Korea. There are some very good tailor shops associated with major hotels, but shops outside the hotels do not always provide good quality work. Sometimes it is especially difficult for western women to have made clothes that fit well. Korean women tend to be both thick- and short-waisted, and Korean tailors tend to make women's clothes that way. Satisfactory fits may require many fitting sessions, and most short-term visitors don't have the time. Taking fabrics home is usually a wiser course.

One does not go to Korea to shop for clothes and fabric, even though both can be good buys there. More strikingly Korean are the furniture and ceramics, both old and new, that are widely available. The country is especially famous for its brass-appointed chests and its celadon ceramics. Both of these items are intensely sought after, and therefore quite expensive. But both, at their best, are exquisitely beautiful and worth their high prices.

Furniture Most people want antique Korean chests because already impressive pieces are made even more attractive by the patina of age. Unfortunately for the neophyte collector, the old pieces have largely been bought up and shipped out. It is now very difficult to find authentic antique chests at any but very, very high prices. Some are available as a result of sales of private holdings or the rare discovery of a small cache here and there, but most real antiques are off the market.

Fortunately, South Korea has a prosperous and accomplished modern chest-making industry that manufactures some very fine products. The best of the modern chests are made from properly cured wood and high-grade brass. They are not cheap, either in cost or quality, but they are often very good alternatives to the even more expensive antique pieces. Before such pieces are purchased, shoppers should try to determine for certain that the wood has been properly cured, because if it has not been, the furniture will later crack as it dries out.

Perhaps in no other area is so much caution on the part of the buyer required as in the purchase of Korean chests and other furniture. The demand for antiques is so great, and the prices paid are so high, that fraud is rampant. A recently made chest that might sell for the equivalent of US$800–1,000, can easily bring US$3,000 or more if it can be passed off as an antique. A piece that is 30 years old might sell for twice as much if the buyer can be convinced that it is 100 years old or more. This creates an atmosphere in which *caveat emptor* is not just a caution, but a requirement.

How does the novice protect himself or herself? Buying from well-established dealers who advertise their wares is one way; the more public the activities of such people, the less likely they are to be fraudulent. Asking Korean friends for assistance is a good step, since if they themselves are not expert, they often know someone who is. Studying the market oneself, long before purchases are made, might be the best protection against fraud.

However, the potential buyer should always be skeptical of beautiful antiques offered at low prices. Korean chests are sought after worldwide, and there are always foreign and domestic buyers keeping track of shop inventories and estate sales. The likelihood that the professionals have missed a great bargain is very slim. It is much more likely that an unscrupulous dealer is trying to make a fast buck. Many excellent pieces are to be had, but not at bargain basement prices, no matter what story a seller may spin.

Ceramics

The situation in the celadon market is similar, but not as extreme. Old celadon pieces can be really old, over one thousand years, and that is much harder to fake than the 100 or so years required to make a chest old. On the other hand, a really well preserved piece of celadon will not look all that different from a relatively new piece to the non-expert.

To further complicate matters, Korean potters have spent untold hours, energy and money trying to replicate the great celadon masterpieces of earlier centuries, with great success in many cases. The skill and care of these craftsmen is of such high quality that the purchase by anybody but a museum curator or the most avid of collectors of an antique piece rather than a more recent one does not make much sense.

The highest quality new pieces cost very large sums – US$5,000 is not unusual – so they represent investment enough for most people.

In fact, this obsession by contemporary South Korean ceramics artists with reproducing the work of the past is decidedly a mixed blessing. Much of their work is remarkably good, not just beautiful and authentic looking, but also based on meticulous research and clever analysis of the elements necessary to copy the old pieces. Some craftsmen have discovered things about the clays and glazes used in the past that had not been known before. Their dedication to the task is as impressive as their skill at shaping and finishing the ceramic pieces with which they work.

So much time and effort go into copying the past, however, that contemporary ceramic work in South Korea can almost not be called an art, since the creative and imaginative elements that are necessary for art are often lacking. A great many of Korea's potters are concerned only with reproducing the past, rather than with building on the past to forge ahead into new areas of creativity. The work of these people is doubtlessly magnificent to look at and a pleasure to own, but it has a certain sterility.

Many of the craftsmen and artists working in this area have the training and the skill to do more creative work. In fact, many of them were at one time creative artists of one sort or another. But the adoration of the past, a powerful tendency in all Korean art forms, directs talented people toward doing over again what has been done well in the past. The influence of Confucianism is apparent here, as is the weakness of artistic individualism in Korea.

Be that as it may, Korean ceramics are beautiful and available. Seoul, especially, has a large number of shops selling modern copies of the masterpieces of the past. They come in a wide variety of sizes, shapes and colors, but most people find the delicate greens classically associated with celadon the most desirable. Pieces range from small tea and *soju* cups to large vases; tea sets (with five cups, because the Chinese character for four is similar to the character for death, and therefore considered bad luck) are also favorite items.

Another reason to buy new ceramics rather than take a chances with the older pieces is that certain items – almost anything from the Shilla period (57 BC to 935 AD) or earlier, genuine Koryo celadon, and others – cannot be taken from the country without written permission from the central government's Cultural Properties Preservation Bureau. A great many Koreans feel that, in the past, their country has been robbed of many of its cultural relics, so serious steps are taken to preserve those which remain. It is a good idea to save receipts for all ceramics purchased, old and new, to be able to prove one's right to take them out upon departure.

Jewelry

The best semi-precious stones available in Korea are, as previously mentioned, amethyst, smoky topaz and jadite, all of which are mined in the country. Special settings are available from skilled Korean jewelers at reasonable prices, but the quality of stones varies greatly and prices with them. Jadite is not the same as jade, being softer and not as rich in tone as the precious, real jade. Beautifully carved pieces of jadite are available in Korea at reasonable prices.

Novices in the field of jade should not shop for it in Korea, where shop keepers have a tendency to call any green stone jade. Real jade, especially antique pieces from China or Burma, will not be found in the country at bargain prices for much the same reasons that cheap antique chests are not available. Jade is a highly sought after stone, especially the old, exquisitely carved pieces from China; experts know the Asian market so well that good deals are extremely rare.

Brassware

Brassware is all over the place in Korea. The older items are very good quality, heavy brass that improves with age. The newer stuff is inferior in quality, much lighter weight, and lacks the richness and heft of the good things. Bells, lamps, ducks, swans and a great variety of other decorative items are the favorite purchases of foreigners. Almost none of the things now available so widely is good quality, and the prices seem good only because the quality is so low. Older pieces will be expensive, but usually worth it.

One caution on brassware: it is very heavy, and often awkward to pack in luggage. If it is purchased by tourists, they should arrange to have the shop in which it is purchased ship the items home. Most of the better shops will provide this service, and it will make traveling home a lot easier.

Ginseng   Ginseng is a very popular root in Korea, China and Japan, and Korean ginseng is reputed to be the best in the world. It comes in the form of tea, powder, slices and whole roots. It is basically thought of as a medicine, although of the form already discussed; that is, not a time- and symptom-specific treatment, but a general health aid, similar to food supplements or vitamins.

No one has ever been able to demonstrate convincingly that ginseng does, in fact, provide any health benefits. But as with so many other medicines, if users think it helps, then it does. This, too, is an acquired taste, because most visitors find it to be, if not offensive, then at least not very tasty. The tea has a very earthy taste, and smells of dirt. But a great many Koreans swear by it, so it is definitely worth a try. Korean ginseng is highly valued in most Asian countries and by Koreans and Chinese who live outside their native countries. The convenient packets of tea make, therefore, excellent gifts for tourists to take home to Asian friends, especially the older ones.

Other   Purchases in Korea do not have to be expensive. A
souvenir   wide variety of typically Korean items are available at
suggestions very reasonable prices. For instance, dolls dressed in traditional court or peasant clothing are widely available in different sizes and a range of prices. Fans decorated with the famous yin and yang symbol painted in brilliant reds, blues and yellows are inexpensive and attractive. Wooden carved ducks, typically given as wedding gifts in Korea, may also be had for little money.

Seoul has five major shopping areas for tourists and foreigners in general: the department stores, Mary's Alley, Itaewon and the two open markets of South Gate and East Gate. Each of these areas has specialties that make them worth a visit by the dedicated shopper.

Where to shop

The department stores are not great places to shop, although the newer ones, designed and owned by Japanese companies, are state of the art: indoor fountains which dance to canned music, impressive walls of video monitors with computerized displays of the latest in music videos, and bright lights, bright colors and open spaces. The Japanese have built similar establishments in their own country, in Hong Kong, and elsewhere.

Department stores

While worth seeing for themselves, these stores do not offer especially good bargains. But they are useful, from the tourist's point of view, as places to see and price the sorts of things that are available in the country, especially clothing. For the longer-term foreign resident, department stores provide the same things in Korea that they do anywhere else: convenient one-stop shopping, reliable quality and a wide range of choice. All the major stores have sections, entire floors in some cases, that specialize in food, eat in and take-away; this makes them interesting places in which to sample different kinds of restaurants and fast food outlets.

Mary's Alley (Insa-dong), located not far from the American and the Japanese embassies, is still one of the best places to look for antiques. The growing market for these items has led to significant expansion in the number of outlets for antiques in Seoul, but Mary's Alley is one of the oldest. It offers a wide variety of ceramics, furniture, paintings, screens and various smaller items. Old coins, stamps, household items, toys, swords and knives, and a number of other intriguing things are available in the many shops in and around Mary's Alley.

Mary's Alley

Prices in Mary's Alley are high, but in most of the shops quality is good, and the merchants are reliable.

Bargaining is expected, and most of the shops have staff members who can speak one or more foreign languages; all the shops can handle English, most Japanese, and many can manage to deal in French or German as well. Probably the greatest attractions of Mary's Alley as an antiques center are the proximity of so many shops and the merchants' general familiarity with selling to foreigners. It is not, however, exclusively a tourists' shopping area; a great many Koreans buy antiques and works of art here also.

Itaewon   Itaewon is the area of Seoul adjacent to the large American military base in the midst of the city. As recently as the early 1980s, it was primarily known as a center for bars, prostitution and shoddy goods. It was not considered a particularly safe place, and was avoided by respectable people. Now all this has changed.

Shops in Itaewon have been considerably improved in both appearance and goods. It has become a major outlet for factory overruns and seconds, especially for luggage, ready-made clothing and athletic shoes. New and better antique and brassware shops have opened and the older ones have also, in many cases, been spruced up. In general, prices are as low as anywhere else in the country for similar quality goods. Itaewon now has a very good reputation as a shopping area, rivaling similar centers in Hong Kong and Taiwan.

Best buys in Itaewon depend to a certain extent on what overruns are available at any given time, but usually ready-made clothes (cotton and synthetic, especially men's casual shirts and pants), athletic shoes and canvas luggage are good deals, and quite often down jackets and coats can be had at very low prices. Children's clothing is also a good buy in Itaewon. All of these items will have been originally manufactured for export, ending up in Itaewon for various reasons. Buyers of such things should check to make certain that, if the outlet sells seconds, the flaws are not major ones.

Brassware and eelskin products are also very popular in Itaewon. The brass, as mentioned earlier, is now not of nearly as high quality as it used to be, but among the immense variety of forms offered, something is bound to appeal to almost anyone. Most of the brass shops in Itaewon will arrange to ship things so that the customer doesn't have to lug them around during the trip home. Eelskin wallets and purses are specialties of the country, but they range in quality from good to poor, so potential buyers should inspect them carefully.

The last shopping areas of general interest in Seoul are the two large markets of East Gate and South Gate (so-called because of their proximity to the old gates of the former walled city). East Gate is the larger of the two, and may perhaps be one of the largest such market places in Asia. It is dominated by huge, two- and three-story buildings which house thousands of shop and stalls. South Gate is characterized by innumerable street vendors and shops that open into streets and alleys. But in both, much of the action is in the open. *East Gate and South Gate*

Both places are very, very crowded; usually only Korean is spoken; and haggling takes place, although it is declining in importance. Neither is a place to which expensive jewelry should be worn, and purses and pockets should be securely protected against intrusion. Both are also vast and complicated; first-time visitors should either go with someone who knows the market or pay close attention to entry and exit points. It is very easy to get lost in the maze of shops, stalls, alleyways and phenomenally congested streets.

These markets are fascinating places. The atmosphere is charged with hustle and bustle, the workers and customers alike rush and dart with their loads from stall to stall. Each has smells and sights (East Gate particularly gives a rich view of the foodstuffs of Korea) that will enthrall tourists who have never seen this sort of open-air market.

Korean products are usually the best buys in these two markets: dishes, cooking utensils, *ibol* and *yo*, material, sundry household and workshop items. South Gate is an especially good place to buy fresh flowers and plants. Both have repair shops of various sorts, and shops that sell almost anything the western mind can imagine and a great many things it cannot.

Even if one has no intention of buying anything, at least one of these markets should be visited just for the experience. Actually few people can wander around either of them for long without finding something they want. But the smells, sights and sounds are the real treat for foreigners. It is in places like these that the majority of Koreans shop, so they provide an authentic view of daily life.

Leisure and entertainment

For variety of entertainment and cultural activities, South Korea has a great deal to offer. Traditional Korean music, dance, drama and festivals are obviously available, although now very much fading forms that survive largely by government subsidies. But the country also has a strong interest in western musical and dramatic forms, especially classical music and plays. In addition, more modern, less exalted forms of entertainment thrive in Korea: television, night clubs, movies and sports.

Particularly in Seoul, there are plenty of activities to keep the most dedicated busy, although tickets to major events are sometimes hard to come by. Small theater, often run by students and young dissidents, is widespread in the capital city and in other major cities also. Dance companies, small and in some cases not of professional quality, can also be found. There are many art galleries which support the works of local artists and those from elsewhere in the country.

Television

Let's start with the lowest common denominator, television. After nearly 20 years of only black-and-white broadcasts, South Korea got color television in 1980. Television sets are nearly everywhere, no matter how remote a household may be. The government-run television stations have invested considerable amounts of money in building transmission facilities and booster stations to insure that television is available throughout the nation; no mean achievement in a country that has so much of its land area covered by mountains.

While the government may have had political motives for this effort to provide television reception to all, one important impact has been cultural, rather than political. Television in South Korea has served as a force for national unity by providing all people in the country with a standard cultural fare in a standard national language, thus lessening the importance of regional dialects. It has increased the influence of Seoul on national culture because most original programming generates from the capital city.

The fare offered on Korean television varies in quality, of course, but at its best it is very good. Some of the better programs are interesting to foreigners as a source of insight into the way Koreans think and act. Two particular types of show are especially informative along these lines: evening soap operas and police programs. The Korean versions of both have special qualities that distinguish them from their western counterparts.

Soap operas   Soap operas come in two forms, comic and serious. The comic ones focus on the difficulties and confusions of daily living, rarely making any grand points or suggesting social injustice, political ineptitude or anything else of a weighty nature. Mostly they are just funny, and if foreigners want to find out what Koreans think is comical, they should watch some of these shows. Not knowing the language can cause people to miss some of the subtler points, but humor can usually be understood without language.

These comic offerings are also interesting to foreigners because they focus closely on the small details of daily life. Shopping, preparing meals, taking care of kids, dealing with bureaucracy and coping with life in general are the subjects used to generate laughs. Foreigners who otherwise have little chance to enter Korean households can learn a lot from these shows by observing the detail.

Serious soaps on Korean television are a real treat. The story lines are not as complicated as in American soaps, and neither do they run for year after year with elaborate intertwining of unrelated events. Most serious Korean soaps are relatively short – 20 or 30 episodes – and all have to do with the rise and fall (usually the fall) of a family. These stories, like Korea itself, are very much family centered, although with none of the dynastic qualities of things like 'Dallas'.

While rarely focusing on the poor, Korean soaps are not populated by the extraordinarily rich either. Mostly they are about the reasonably well-off, upper-middle classes.

Heartbreak and illness are the main elements of the serious soaps, with black sheep and skeletons in the closet not far behind. Scandal is not an important element, and none of the seamy aspects of stories are baldly presented; rather they are hinted at and referred to obliquely. In part, this is because Korea is a very puritanical society, and the government exercises strict censorship over sexual matters. Very little is made explicit in these shows.

However, a lack of explicitness does not mean a lack of emotion. Korean soap operas can match profound emotion with those of any other country. In fact, weeping and depression, anger and remorse, sadness and tragedy are the very stuff of these shows, and in this they are much like similar shows of the West. What sets them apart is a mode of behavior – shared by Koreans with the Japanese and Chinese – which includes a very physical expression of emotion.

Collapsing to the floor, drooping physiques, hanging heads, wailing and gnashing of teeth are standard behavior. Strong emotions are expressed openly and clearly; private distress is not borne stoically. This is almost as true of the male characters as the female, surprisingly enough. Actually, this extreme activity makes it easier for people who do not know Korean to follow the action.

One of the more disconcerting aspects of Korean soap operas is that the television stations each have a stable of actors who work in every show. So the man who plays a woman's husband in one show may be her brother in the next and then her illicit lover in the next. This changing of roles can be confusing to someone trying to follow the action without understanding the language.

Detective serials

Police programs on Korean television also lack the explicitness of their western counterparts: there is little violence, less blood and not even much crime, at least not on screen. Rather these shows tend to be procedurals, focusing on the nitty-gritty of police work, and they always have a very bluntly made moral: crime doesn't pay. The policemen are usually not pretty boys, although they are played by people considered handsome by Korean standards.

As with the soaps, so with the police shows; no effort is made to keep up with changing fashions in behavior, to excuse criminality or to explain away crime as a result of environmental factors. The criminals are not always portrayed as evil but they are always shown to be misguided, and the cops are always honest. Simple as all this may sound, maybe even simple-minded, the police shows can be very good. They are usually very tightly directed; they are almost all shot on the streets; and they work at verisimilitude.

One of the things that adds considerably to the police shows is the camera work. In fact, a great many of the shows on Korean television are character-ized by excellent camera work, even the rather tiresome variety shows that fill far too many hours of broadcasting time. For many years, television camera-men and their directors in Korea have made very skillful use of multi-camera shots, fades, overlays, color mixing, split screens and windows to provide imaginative pictures of subjects that are not always so captivating.

Other programs Beyond these things, Korean television hasn't much to offer the non-Korean speaker. A lot of sports, mostly soccer and baseball, are aired, and an occa-sional western movie is shown. In the latter case, the movies are usually dubbed rather than subtitled, sometimes with disastrous results. Great voices like those of Gregory Peck, Richard Burton and Law-rence Olivier end up being dubbed by inferior voices, much to the detriment of the movies.

A special weakness of Korean television is the musical variety shows that are on nearly every night. While the main talent, the solo or lead singer, is often good, the back-up is frequently quite terrible. On-stage bands are often less than mediocre, and the company dancers who appear in nearly every number are neither talented nor well choreographed. This is particularly true on the large number of shows which present pop music: the voices are good, the arrangements usually acceptable, but the musicianship and dancing leave much to be desired. One is tempted to say that Koreans lack rhythm.

All major cities in Korea can receive, in addition to the three Korean stations, the television and radio service of AFKN. For English-speaking visitors, AFKN is perhaps the best source of news and weather reports. The news has a decidedly American bent, of course, but it is uncensored and up to date.

AFKN is not intended to serve anyone but the American military forces in Korea, and it makes no effort to serve anyone else. Nonetheless, its broadcasts can be received by the great majority of Koreans, and it is a very popular source for the study of English. A great many Koreans also appreciate AFKN as a source of news and information that is independent of the Korean government and as a means of keeping up with the fads of English-language pop culture.

AFKN

Koreans can sing. Nearly all educated Koreans have actually received some training in singing; it is a standard part of a good education. Koreans like to sing, and they like to have other people sing. This is an especially important fact for foreigners to keep in mind if they are going to be entertained by business or professional contacts.

Singing

Dinner with a group of Koreans often leads to a request for foreign guests to sing a song. A couple can get away with singing together, but individuals will usually be expected to sing one song each. Those who will be involved in a lot of entertaining with the same group of people might want to work up a couple of songs for these occasions just for variety.

Nothing fancy is expected, and in fact the better known the song, the more it will be appreciated. Patriotic songs always go over well, as do simple humorous ditties. Koreans who have had extensive contacts with foreigners have heard a great many different songs, so they will be familiar with almost anything most people can come up with. No great expertise is required, but a valiant effort to perform an entire piece is much appreciated.

Not just the foreigners are expected to sing. Depending on the amount of alcohol that has been consumed, nearly everyone at the table will eventually contribute. Keep in mind that they have been doing this for years, so if Koreans seem well prepared for their performance, it is because they are. The more daring (and the less sober) might accompany their own song with a dance also, although the foreign guests will not be expected to go this far.

If the Koreans entertaining at such a function consider themselves close enough friends of their guests, the foreigners will almost certainly be taught a Korean song. There are many simple, beautiful Korean songs that can easily be learned in a short time. Having one of them in the repertoire will make a favorable impression on Korean hosts and guests, and performing one in this dinner setting will encourage the Koreans present to join in, thus creating a very pleasant atmosphere.

Some Koreans are, in fact, rather puzzled that their foreign friends cannot or are not readily willing to perform at these gatherings. It is such a natural thing for them, and all are so well prepared to do it, that reluctance and hesitation on the part of outsiders seem strange. Therefore foreign guests who are prepared will put such people at ease.

High culture Seoul has two major complexes in which cultural events take place: the Sejong Cultural Center, located in the heart of town mid-way between City Hall and the Capitol building on Sejong-no, and the National Theater, located in Namsan Park, just south of the city center and quite near the Shilla Hotel. The National Theater has two auditoriums which house the National Ballet, the National and the Seoul Symphony Orchestras, the National Opera Company and several theater companies. The Sejong Cultural Center, which is an impressive piece of architecture, has a year-round schedule of performing arts, including symphony orchestras, solo performers, dance companies, beauty pageants and a wide variety of other things.

Major events at these two sites are very popular, and thus tickets can be extremely hard to come by at short notice. The two English language newspapers published in Seoul, *The Korea Times* and *The Korea Herald*, list current and forthcoming events late in the week, but often this information appears too late to allow time to get tickets for the most popular events. Another publication, *This Week in Seoul*, which is available free at most hotels, prints the same information but poses the same problem.

Hotel service desks can sometimes be helpful in acquiring tickets, although Korean friends and contacts are often an even better bet. Important events are usually announced well in advance by banners which appear in various places in Seoul: the two most common places are on pedestrian overpasses on main streets or on the front of the building which houses the sponsoring company. Tourists interested in attending such events should start the procedure for acquiring tickets as soon as they see an announcement; this will make it more likely that tickets will be available.

Western classical music is very popular in Korea. The country has some magnificent pianists, violinists, and cellists; many of these people have attained international reputations, and now play for major orchestras throughout the world. Both the National and the Seoul Symphony Orchestras are very good, and both play the full range of the western classical repertoire.

Ballet and opera are another matter in Korea. Neither has come close to achieving the levels of excellence that instrumental music has; neither has a season that is nearly as long as those of the symphonies. But both are very popular, with tickets for their performances sometimes as hard to get as tickets for the other events.

Concert halls in Korea pose a special problem in the late fall and winter: they are not very well heated, and Korea is very, very cold in the winter. Sitting still for a couple of hours in one of these halls can chill a person profoundly. The only protection is to dress very warmly, paying particular attention to the feet, which will have to be on cold concrete floors for a long time. Remember that Koreans almost all wear long underwear, beginning early in the fall, so while it may not look like they are warmly dressed, they are.

Movies Korea has a very active movie industry, which produces dozens of new films a year. These films are much like shows made for television, but not quite so restrained and moralistic. Love melodramas are most popular, followed by police and crime stories and historical dramas. In addition non-Korean films, mostly American, are shown throughout the country. The foreign films are a mixture of older and more recent works. Films and show times are available daily in the newspapers.

Seoul has a great many theaters, most of which have several showings a day. Tickets are quite cheap by western standards, with the cheapest seats going for less than US$1, and the most expensive a little over US$2. Most showings are heavily attended, with crowds frequently being made up of a high percentage of students and children.

This last fact sometimes poses a problem for foreigners. Unlike foreign movies shown on television, recent films shown in theaters are usually not dubbed, but subtitled. This means that most of the audience does not have to listen to the dialog to follow the action, they can just read the subtitles. As a result, the audience frequently gets rather talkative during movies. Sometimes theaters get so noisy that patrons who can understand the dialog cannot hear it.

Movies are not a special cultural attraction in Korea. Although the dedicated film buff might find attending a showing or two interesting, only the rare exceptionally good movie will be of more general interest. As with concert halls, so too with movie houses; they can get very cold in the winter. Television and *tabang* are better for learning about Korea and its people.

Baseball is probably the most popular sport in the **Sports** country. Korea is one of few countries in the world with its own professional baseball league. The annual university sports competition in Seoul has baseball games as one of its central events, and the national high school baseball championships are perhaps the most watched sporting event of the year. All three levels of the sport are broadcast on television.

While baseball has increased in popularity since the end of the Korean War, partially as a result of the American influence, the history of baseball in Korea goes back much further in time. It was probably introduced by Christian missionaries from the United States before the turn of the century. Its popularity increased during the Japanese occupation, 1905–45, because it was by that time also a very popular sport in Japan. So the American presence only reinforced an already strong tendency.

Professional baseball started in the early eighties. The teams are owned by large corporations and are based in particular cities. As yet a very young concern, professional baseball has had some growing pains, but it has proven quite popular. The level of play is not up to the standards of the best of the Japanese and American professional leagues, and neither are the salaries paid to the players. It will, however, almost certainly survive and grow in popularity for a number of years, because it is backed by a strong pre-professional network, including university, high school and youth leagues. Thus it is not a professional sport that has been imposed on to Korean culture, but to a great extent grows naturally out of it.

Basketball, volleyball, soccer and boxing are also very popular sports in Korea. The country has during the last 20 years or so produced some very good professional boxers in the lower weight divisions. Company-sponsored and armed forces teams play regular seasons in both men's and women's basketball and volleyball, and their games are frequently televised. Korea has one national professional soccer team, called Arirang, which competes internationally, although not in a regular league.

Golf is popular among a particular set in Korea, namely the well-to-do. Although there are some 20 courses in and around the city of Seoul, they are all clubs requiring stiff membership dues and high green fees. Most tourists will not have ready access to a course, and neither will it be worth while to bring clubs to the country. Unless one has access to the American military courses, which are quite reasonable in price, or a friend in the Korean military – golf is very popular with generals and high-ranking government officials – costs are prohibitive.

Foremost among the more traditional Korean sports is *taekwando*, a martial art form introduced into Korea from China during the Tang Dynasty and later passed on to Japan in a slightly different form. *Taekwando* has in the past decade gained international popularity; it will be included as a demonstration sport in the 1988 Olympics. Many foreigners come to Korea to study *taekwando*, and a great many more take advantage of their time in the country to learn about it. Regular exhibitions of the sport are held at Kukkiwon, the main *taekwando* gymnasium in Seoul.

Since AFKN (radio and television) broadcasts a great deal of American professional and college sports, and the Korean stations carry professional, company team, university and high school sports regularly, sports fans can almost always find something to watch in Korea. It seems very likely that having had the Asian Games in 1986 and with the Olympics looming in 1988 the popularity of sports in Korea will increase, causing old sports to grow and new ones to sprout up.

Holidays and festivals   Korea has two major traditional holidays that are celebrated throughout the country in dedicated fashion, Lunar New Year and Chusok. Both of these are tied to the lunar calendar, and thus their dates fluctuate according to the solar calendar from year to year. Lunar New Year occurs between late January and early March, but usually in February, and Chusok occurs between late August and early October. In addition, Korea has 12 other official holidays, most commemorating specific political or cultural events.

The New Year celebration in Korea is actually a bit of a problem. The official holiday, which is three days long, occurs on 1, 2 and 3 January of the solar calendar. National, provincial and city government offices are closed on these days, as are most large businesses. The government has for years pressured the populace to make this the only New Year celebration, but without notable success. Most people persist in considering the Lunar New Year the more important one. *New Year*

Usually this boils down to both times being celebrated. The official holiday is one that the people will not refuse, of course, but neither will they give up the traditional one. Although government offices are usually officially open during the Lunar New Year period, they are almost always very short staffed. A similar situation exists in the large companies, while small shops generally close up for at least three days, and street vendors disappear for a like time.

Lunar New Year is the most important holiday of the year. It is pre-eminently a period for family get-togethers. Travel on the trains and buses at this time is virtually impossible, because everyone is going home, in that curious sense in which Koreans use that term. They are required by custom to visit their native places, even if they and all their immediate family are from somewhere else.

Chusok, on the other hand, is both an official and a traditional holiday marking the harvest festival and the beginning of fall. It occurs on the fifteenth day of the eighth lunar month, which usually places it ahead of the autumnal equinox of the solar calendar. Chusok is often referred to as the Korean Thanksgiving Day, a reference to the American celebration which occurs in late November. *Chusok*

Staying up all night to observe the full moon is one of the traditional ceremonies of Chusok. Everyone in Korea also marks it with the exchanging of gifts and celebrations with family and friends. Foreigners who are in Korea at the time of Chusok should anticipate both the giving and receiving of gifts. Bonuses are also given to servants, drivers and the like at this time. Gifts of fruit in fancy baskets (these will be available all over the country, beginning some weeks before Chusok) or of imported Scotch or cognac are quite appropriate to give to business and professional contacts.

Hanbok Both the above holidays are treats for foreign visitors to Korea. Especially on Lunar New Year, many Koreans dress up in traditional clothing (called *hanbok*), and entire families go out to parks and palaces. The sartorial display that results is impressive. Men, women and children all dressed in *hanbok* walk the streets together and gather in the parks. Most of these people, especially the men, wear *hanbok* only twice or three times a year so this is an opportunity that does not occur often.

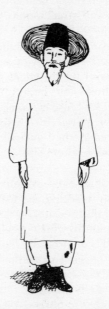

*Old man in traditional dress and horsehair hat (*hanbok*)*
(illustration by Paula Murray)

As has been mentioned earlier, little of traditional Korean culture remains outside government-sponsored showcases. There is nothing wicked or conspiratorial about this, rather the economic and social order that gave rise to and supported the traditional forms has disappeared. Efforts by the government, and by student groups who are independently pursuing similar ends, can only provide temporary and artificial solutions to the problem of a disappearing culture.

Although it is sometimes possible to find traditional forms being practiced in rural villages on special festival days, most forms of traditional culture can only can be seen in places like Korea House and the Folk Village. However, some people have been designated as living national treasures, and occasionally, with the right connections, it is possible to see a performance by them, and thus gain a glimpse of high art forms now nearly gone. One of the most spectacular of these rare items is the famous Korean mask dance drama.

Calling this high art might be a bit of an exaggeration, since if ever an art form was popular, gross, irreverent and hostile to established institutions, it was – and is – Korean mask dance. This drama form came from villagers who lived in an essentially hostile relationship with a little-seen government, whose main association with the villagers was through the tax collector and military recruiter, and in close contact with the spirits of shamanistic folk religions. Mask dance drama is sarcastic, critical, bawdy, spiritual and very, very funny.

All male actors don elaborate masks and play simplistic roles, often aided in their dramatic interpretation by liberal consumption of *makkolli* and *soju*, especially if the weather is cold. There are smart guys and bad guys, cuckold husbands and shrewish wives, venial government bureaucrats, all done in by the common cleverness of simple peasants. The settings are very plain, but the mime and acting is truly impressive. Anyone who ever gets a chance to see this nearly extinct art performed in an authentic village setting should make every effort to do so.

Seoul and the Olympics

Consider for a moment where the 1988 Olympics are being held. Seoul, South Korea, has been a central focus of the post-war conflict between the communist and the non-communist nations. Korea is one of few places in which troops of communist countries and western countries have directly engaged one another since the end of the Second World War. Both North and South Korea are highly armed, hostile countries that face each other across a narrow DMZ that periodically is the site of hot outbreaks of the so-called Cold War.

Recent international incidents Barely five years before the proposed start of the Seoul Olympics, the shooting down of a Korean civilian airliner by Soviet aircraft once again focused world attention on the potential for superpower conflict in the region. Less than three years before the planned opening of the Asian Games in Seoul, the North Korean government plotted and executed a murderous assault on the South Korean president and most of his cabinet in Burma, killing 17, including 4 cabinet members.

Even among its supposed friends, South Korea has been having its political problems lately. In 1983, it outraged sensibilities in Taiwan by jailing, instead of sending to 'freedom' in Taiwan, mainland Chinese nationals who had hijacked an airliner and forced it to fly to South Korea. In 1985, similar incidents involving mainland naval craft and military planes have kept the issue of South Korean relations with Taiwan very much on the front burner.

Relations with the United States, long the staunchest ally of South Korea, have been strained in recent years also. Koreagate, trade issues and international competition for markets have brought these two friends into an adversarial position economically. Complaints from the internal opposition that the United States dominates the South Korean government have complicated matters, and the seizure in 1985 of the United States Information Service library and the American Chamber of Commerce offices in Seoul have made things even more tense. During 1986–7, the increasingly violent student opposition stressed its desire to see US influence reduced or eliminated all together.

Internally, the government faces a vociferous and increasingly popular opposition; parliamentary elections in 1984 yielded a virtual clean sweep for the opposition in Seoul, Pusan and other large cities; only the disproportionate representation given to rural constituencies and the power to appoint representatives kept the ruling party a majority. A huge international debt has made a great many Koreans nervous about the stability of their economy and the prospects for future growth. Declining exports, sluggish growth and the collapse of large conglomerates, including the nation's sixth largest – the Kukje Group – late in 1984, have fueled these concerns.

Domestic problems

Not only does South Korea have its problems, but the international Olympics movement has not been doing too well lately either. The summer Olympics of 1980 in Moscow and 1984 in Los Angeles saw boycotts by one or other of the major world power blocs. The United States and many of its allies stayed away from Moscow to protest about the Soviet invasion of Afghanistan, and the Soviet bloc reciprocated the favor, giving much vaguer reasons, in 1984. The image of the Olympic movement as an agency of international peace and unity was considerably tarnished. Having the 1988 Games in a Cold-War focal point like Seoul hardly seems calculated to polish it up.

The Olympic movement

There is no question that the Seoul Olympics are a gamble. South Korea is investing a great deal of money in the Games and perhaps even more of its reputation as a nearly developed society. The loss of face that a disastrous Games would bring to the country would become a significant factor in its politics for some time to come, and the centrifugal forces of regionalism would probably be strengthened. In the provinces, there is already considerable resentment about the amount of money being spent on Seoul when other parts of the nation need development funds. If the Olympics are not a success, this resentment will become a political liability for the government.

The International Olympic Committee (IOC) has also committed a great deal to the Seoul Olympics. By choosing a controversial site, the IOC has created a situation in which the communist bloc nations could once again stage a counter-Olympics, as they did in 1984. A second occurrence would be a severe blow to the international quality of the Games. Were this to happen for the third time in a row a significant part of the international sports community would be missing from the Games. It is entirely possible that such a step would mark the end of the international Olympic movement as it now exists.

Why Seoul?   If all this is true, why did Seoul bid for and why did the IOC grant it the 1988 Games? The formal answer to the second part of this question is that Seoul put forward the most convincing bid. It promised most and gave evidence of being able to deliver most (a most much strengthened by Seoul's performance during the Asian Games). It had the unqualified support of the national government, and could draw on the reputation of South Korea as a country that produces to persuade the IOC that Seoul should be selected over the other competing cities. Maybe the fact that the citizens of Seoul had no way short of street riots to reject the Olympics, in contrast to other potential sites, made a difference also.

However, rejection was not on many minds in South Korea in 1981, when the announcement of the site for 1988 was made. Even those people who, at the time, could analyze the potential cost to the country and to their particular region were caught up in the fervor that surrounded the bid. For Seoul to win was for the nation to win, and nearly everyone saw it that way. The fact that the other leading contender for selection was a Japanese city made the competition more important. For many, beating the Japanese was far more significant than winning the Olympics.

Response to the announcement was virtually unanimous: pride in all cases, unrestrained joy in most. To a person, South Koreans saw Seoul's selection as an indication that the entire country had, in some ill-defined way, arrived, made it, achieved significant status. Probably no other single thing could have captured so powerfully this sense of accomplishment as did being awarded the Olympics. In a very real way for all citizens of the South it gave focus to the discipline, the sacrifice and the ordeal of the previous 30 years, providing a sense of redemption.

It must be emphasized here, very clearly, that this was the reaction of the moment; but nonetheless real for being momentary, in fact, quite the opposite. The selection of Seoul as the Olympic site spoke to

Reproduced by kind permission of *The Asian Wall Street Journal*

profound sensibilities in the people of South Korea that had little to do with transient and provincial issues. The harshest critics of the central government, the most extreme nationalists of the student protest movement, had to pause for a time to reflect on the symbolic importance of this event.

Time has brought many people in the country to a different view of the Olympics. It is easy, when in the opposition, to condemn even the true achievements of the ruling powers. It is also easy to pose obstacles to the goals of the government. But in sober moments, even the most extreme of the opposition must admit that the selling of South Korea as a place in which the Olympics may take place is a major achievement which legitimizes, if not the ruling powers, then certainly the indomitable spirit of the Korean people who, in the face of overwhelming odds, have made their country into a modern marvel.

Actually, at the time Seoul was granted the Olympic Games, none of the major problems mentioned earlier had arisen. The shooting down of the airliner, the bombing in Rangoon, the decline in Korea's economic position and the re-emergence of violent student and worker opposition all came after the site announcement. In 1982, South Korea had just come through a very difficult period of political instability, beginning with the assassination of Park Chung Hee in 1979 and including the uprising in Kwangju in 1980 that drove the government out of the city for weeks. After the fall of Kwangju, the government of Chun Doo Hwan was firmly in control of the country, and economically things were going well.

Hosting the Games is not just a grandstand play for the government, although it will be a great opportunity to show off the country's achievements. Two more substantial goals are sought: first, to reduce tensions on the Korean peninsula, and second, to use the Asian Games and the Olympics to provide the momentum to boost the country's economy from the intermediate stage into full development.

The first of these goals will be the more difficult to achieve, largely because it depends on the cooperation of several other countries. The United States, the Soviet Union, China and, above all else, North Korea will determine whether or not the Olympics serve the cause of peace and stability or continue to reflect the international tensions that have marred the Summer Games in the past.

North–South tensions

North Korea may be the key to this, and its initial reaction was not especially promising: Pyongyang denounced the selection of Seoul as a 'sinister plot to create two Koreas'. The Soviet Union suggested to the IOC that the participation of the Soviet bloc might be guaranteed if some events were to be held in North Korea, and with this backing the North has presented various proposals for venues to be shifted away from Seoul. Late in 1986, the South Korean government made some concessions, but the two sides were still far apart. It now seems certain that, if the 1988 Olympics are held in Korea at all, some events will be staged in the North, although no agreement on which or how many has yet been reached.

Early in 1987, it still seems that the Soviet Union is planning to attend the Seoul Games. Soviet and East European athletes have even appeared in South Korea for the first time, at ice skating exhibitions, thus raising hopes for communist bloc cooperation in 1988. After achieving significant successes in the Asian Games, China is even more determined to appear in Seoul, and the mutual hostility of Seoul and Beijing has been somewhat lessened by recent events.

If the North finds itself confronted with Soviet and Chinese commitments to go to Seoul, most of the bargaining power for its getting a larger role will be gone. North Korea has undercut itself by acts like the Rangoon bombing, but *pro forma* support from the Soviets, Cuba and the Eastern European countries probably will be given. South Korea, having made some concessions, is in a fairly strong position to resist further maneuvering by the North.

Other steps by the North Koreans might create even greater problems for Seoul. Both sides have periodically perpetrated acts of violence against the other, with the North being more active recently. If terrorist acts were to increase in frequency in South Korea prior to the Games, the communist bloc would have a convenient excuse for pulling out. Given North Korea's bellicosity and xenophobia, nearly anything is possible.

However, if South Korea can pull off the participation of both East and West, and also secure the participation of the North Koreans, the Games will serve the cause of peace and stability. Seoul will be able to claim credit for restoring the international aspect of the Olympics, while at the same time demonstrating South Korea's ability to get along with ideological opponents. And all visiting nations will see the development of the country.

Plan for growth

As for the economic goals of staging the Games, South Korea has looked to Japan as a model. This argument contends that the 1964 Olympics re-established Japan's international reputation after the Second World War, and also provided it with the impetus to become the economic giant it is today. The 1988 Games should do similar things for South Korea. Having the world see the country with its best face on will bring it to the attention of millions of people who have thought little of it before. A widely held view of South Korea as a small, poor, dependent country will dissolve under the lights of televised Games.

This sort of exposure, it is hoped, will elevate the nation's international image, and thereby generate investment, purchase of goods and trade relations. This new stimulus is just what the nation's rapidly growing economy needs to become a major factor in the world, the argument concludes.

Olympic sites

Whatever the merits of this argument, the South Korean central and Seoul city governments are doing their share to stimulate the economy by spending the equivalent of US$1.4 billion to upgrade existing and construct new facilities. The centerpiece is a magnificent new stadium which seats 100,000 people, and is part of the already completed Seoul Sports Complex, just south of the Han River. It is here that the opening and closing ceremonies and track and field competition for the Olympic Games will be held.

In addition to the main stadium, the Seoul Sports Complex has two other general-use stadiums, an indoor pool and a baseball stadium. All are to be used for sports and for many of the cultural events that are planned for the Games. Not only does it provide first-class venues for events, but the Seoul Sports Complex is also very conveniently located only 30 minutes from the heart of town, and is served by a sparkling clean subway line that can accommodate 180,000 people per hour if necessary.

The National Sports Complex is 4 km away, and was completed early in 1986. This includes a velodrome which seats 6,000 for cycling events, 3 more gymnasiums and an additional swimming pool which meets the Olympic requirement of seating for at least 10,000 spectators. Gymnastics, cycling, weightlifting, swimming and diving events will be held here. The National Sports Complex can also be reached via the subway.

A fully equipped shooting range, where the 42nd World Shooting Championships were staged in 1978, is located in northeastern Seoul. Construction on an Olympic yachting marina began in 1983 in the southern port city of Pusan; work on it is ahead of schedule. Finally, the rowing and canoeing events will

SEOUL SIDELINE   BY   HUNG MO GWAI

Reproduced by kind permission of *The Asian Wall Street Journal* be held on the Han River in Seoul. The stands at this site hold 25,000 people and were completed early in 1986.

As the city also hosted the Asian Games two years before the Olympics all the facilities had to be finished by then, so Seoul's Olympic Organizing Committee does not expect that there will be a last-minute flurry of construction to get ready for the Olympics. In fact, one of the most persuasive parts of the bid package offered to the IOC was the advanced state of construction of the Seoul Sports Complex in 1981. More than any other single element, this convinced the IOC that Seoul would be ready for the 1988 Games if granted to them. Many of the difficulties that complicated the 1976 Games in Montreal, the 1972 Games in Munich and the 1968 Games in Mexico City will be avoided in Seoul in 1988 because the sites will be ready early.

Finance The Los Angeles Games in 1984 were run for surprisingly little money and turned a tidy profit for the Los Angeles Olympic Organizing Committee, while costing the city of Los Angeles, the state of California and the federal government of the United States relatively little. The same will not be true for the Seoul Games; no one intends that the Games themselves will make any money. The national prestige that is involved guarantees that Seoul city and the central government will make herculean efforts to have the Games succeed.

An additional US$1.6 billion will be needed to pay for actually organizing and staging the Games, above and beyond the cost of constructing facilities. The organizers hope that most of these costs will be covered by sale of television rights, sponsorship and licensing agreements, lotteries, ticket sales and the sale of commemorative coins and stamps. If these steps garner enough money, then the Seoul city and central governments will only be out of pocket for the construction costs.

So far some parts of this strategy seem to be working very well. Two major multinational corporations, Coca-Cola and Eastman Kodak, have already shelled out a reported US$15 million each for official sponsor status; and, by mid-November 1985, more than 70 countries had paid a total of over US$100 for sponsorship. This exceeded the amount hoped for by some US$20 million.

A disappointing setback occurred when the American television network NBC won the bidding war for broadcast rights for a guaranteed US$300 million. Although the final amount could go as high as US$500 million if all goes well, it would still be more than US$200 million less than the Koreans had hoped for. The bids were not as high as expected primarily because of the 14-hour time difference between South Korea and the east coast of the United States, making prime-time viewing hours and the times of major events hard to coordinate.

Nonetheless, both fiscally and physically, Seoul is almost certain to make the Games work. When problems can be solved by discipline, hard work and planning, Koreans can handle them easily. The potentially more difficult obstacles to the Games are political: participation of the Soviet bloc nations, the attitude and actions of North Korea and the South's own significant internal problems **The way ahead**

Here the South has yet to prove itself, though it is making sincere efforts. Recent overtures to the North, including accepting flood disaster aid in the spring of 1985 and cooperating in family visit exchanges in the fall, show that the Chun government is trying to learn to live with the North. Visits of Soviet bloc athletes, who were greeted by a display of the Soviet flag for the first time ever in the South, promise to make participation in the Games by the Soviets and their allies more likely.

These problems are far from resolved. World events could yet make it difficult for the communist states to attend an Olympics in a vociferously anti-communist country that they see as a toady of the American imperialists. North Korea is notoriously unpredictable and mysterious. Kim Il Sung is apparently nearing the end of his days, and no one can guess what steps he and his country might be willing to take to prevent the South from achieving a major propaganda coup like the Olympics. In the first half of 1987, the internal political problems of the South became even more serious and challenged the Chun regime in new ways.

However, if South Korea can survive the downing by the Soviets of a commercial Korean airliner and the bombing of its president and most of his cabinet in Rangoon by North Korean thugs, then it must be said that it is at least making a major effort. As in so many other things, South Korea is not in direct control of all the issues that may turn the 1988 Olympics into a failure. It is gambling that, for once, results will count more than words and gestures, and that the Games will succeed despite the world's inability to live at peace with itself.

Attending the Games

Like the Asian Games, the Olympics coincide with the fall, Korea's most beautiful season. Chusok occurs in the middle of events, giving foreign visitors a marvelous opportunity to enjoy the country's most charming holiday. The Games themselves are sufficient justification for going anywhere, and Korea needs no extra features to justify a visit by anyone. Getting both South Korea and the Olympics in one trip is a real bonus.

For almost everyone, Seoul will be the place to be during the Olympics. All venues except yachting will be close enough to the city to make them relatively easy to get to. The majority of events – track and field, swimming, gymnastics, wrestling, volleyball and others – will be accessible from the major downtown hotels via the subway. This should make it possible for the masses of people attending to move around with relative ease.

No one should plan to travel from hotels to events on the surface streets except by shuttle vans and buses. Private cars will most likely not be allowed near the sites, and parking is already extremely difficult to come by even without the Olympics. Special transportation arrangements will be provided to the remoter sites, including shooting and rowing and canoeing, but even these are not much more than an hour away from downtown.

Those visitors who want deluxe-class accommodation and maximum convenience should try for the Lotte, Chosun or Seoul Plaza hotels, or only a little bit less luxury can be had at the President and Koreana. All five of these hotels are very conveniently located for travel to the Olympic sites by subway. The number two subway line connects downtown with the Olympic complex; from these hotels the Shichong or Ulchiro-ipku stops will be convenient with the Seoul Sports Complex stop as the primary goal at the other end. But the other major luxury hotels – the Shilla, Hilton, Hyatt Regency and Sheraton Walker Hill – will almost certainly provide convenient transportation to make up for the fact that they are not located close to subway stops.

Actually, of course, most people will have to take what they can get. Major hotels have long been fully booked by travel agents for tour groups that will come to South Korea on package deals covering air fare, accommodation, Olympic tickets and internal transportation. Trying to make private arrangements became difficult even as early as two years in advance.

In fact, hotel space will probably be at a premium during the Olympics. The Seoul Organizing Committee estimates that 18,000 hotel rooms will be required for the Games, and at present the city has not quite 12,000; hotels currently under construction and planned for completion by 1988 will add only about another 1,200 rooms. The Seoul city government hopes to make up some of the shortfall by offering several million dollars in low interest loans to *yogwan* to allow them to upgrade to acceptable international standards. But even if fully successful, this plan will provide not quite enough rooms.

Despite the many potential difficulties, foreigners with long experience of South Korea will not be surprised to see the Olympics come off without any major problems. The country is justly renowned for its discipline and ability to deliver. Some years ago, Seoul managed to stage the Miss Universe pageant while students protested loudly within a few blocks of the auditorium where the festivities were being held; the huge international television audience had no idea anything was wrong. The Asian Games in late

1986 were also conducted without any significant disruptions. Potential visitors to the Olympics in South Korea can therefore rest assured that, if international and internal tensions do not forestall the Seoul Games, the investment in time and money necessary to attend them will pay off richly.

Map

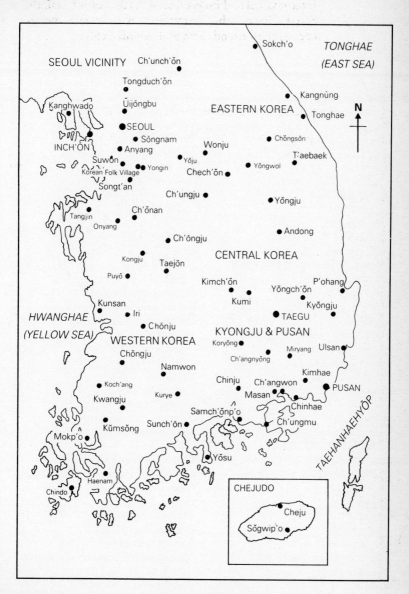

Main towns of Korea

Index

Index by Meg Davies

Suggestions

This page can be used to send in your suggestions for improving the book. What vital matters have been overlooked? What difficulties and pitfalls have been neglected or glossed over? What else should the intending visitor know about the quirks of the Korean way of life? Please write and tell us.

If your suggestions are adopted in any future edition, you will receive a free copy in recognition of your services in helping other people cope with Korea.

Please send your suggestions to Gary Steenson, c/o Basil Blackwell Ltd, 108 Cowley Road, Oxford OX4 1JE.

Name ....

Address ....

My suggestions are